DR. FRANCIS T. STRIBLING
AND MORAL MEDICINE

DR. FRANCIS T. STRIBLING AND MORAL MEDICINE

Curing the Insane at Virginia's Western State Hospital: 1836-1874

Alice Davis Wood

GallileoGianniny Publishing

Copyright © 2004, 2005 by Alice Davis Wood.

Library of Congress Number:		2004091922
ISBN :	Hardcover	1-4134-4981-6
	Softcover	1-4134-4980-8

This book was printed in the United States of America.

To order additional copies of this book, contact:
Xlibris Corporation
1-888-795-4274
www.Xlibris.com
Orders@Xlibris.com
22694

CONTENTS

LIST OF IMAGES

CHAPTER 5—Contention between
Western State and Eastern State

CHAPTER 6—Stribling and Dix: An
intense friendship

CHAPTER 10—Civil War

APPENDIX D—Additional figures

Very respectfully y[...]
Fran^s T. Stribling

Dr. FRANCIS T. STRIBLING,
PHYSICIAN AND SUP'T OF THE WESTERN LUNATIC ASYLUM

IMAGE 1

Dr. Francis T. Stribling.
(Courtesy, University of Virginia Library.)

When does a man so urgently require the aid of a
    rational fellow being
To guide his footsteps, as when he wanders thus in
    mental darkness?
Or when does he so much need the knowledge and
    guidance of others,
As when his own mind is a wild chaos
Agitated by passions that he cannot quell,
And haunted by forms of terror
Which the perverted energy of his nature
Is perpetually calling into being, but cannot disperse.

                    Francis T. Stribling, 1838. (i)

INTRODUCTION

B y focusing on the experiences and achievements of Dr. Francis T. Stribling, this book recounts the professional biography of a remarkable figure: the first graduate of the University of Virginia medical school; the second superintendent of Western State Hospital for thirty-eight years; the author of a substantial revision to the Virginia state law governing the diagnosis and care of the insane; a long-time friend and advisor to social reformer Dorothea Dix; one of the thirteen founders of the association that later became the American Psychiatric Association; and one of the earliest and most influential proponents of Moral Medicine in the American South.

Dr. Francis Stribling's long, influential commitment to advancing the care and cure of the mentally ill is not widely known, an obscurity this book hopes to correct. His history, however, is inseparable from the history of Western State Hospital, and so the book offers, also, a detailed description of that institution's early history and practices. And finally, because Dr. Stribling's history and that of the institution he headed for nearly four decades were influenced—as all personal and institutional lives must be—by significant events and attitudes of their time, the story of Francis Stribling and

Western State Hospital is also, in microcosm, a story of 19th-century psychiatry, 19th-century disputes about race, gender, and class, and 19th century politics (particularly those of the American Reconstruction.)

CHAPTER 1

The Early Years

F rancis Taliaferro Stribling was born on January 20, 1810 in Augusta County, Virginia, [1] a region in the Shenandoah Valley that had been claimed for England under the first Virginia charter.[2] His father, Erasmus Stribling, practiced law in Staunton and served as the town's mayor as well as the clerk of the Augusta County court. Stribling's mother Matilda was the only child of Jacob Kinney, who had arrived in Augusta County in the late 1780s and became one of the area's wealthiest and most influential men.[3]

Stribling's father built a resort near Staunton in 1817 and named it Stribling Springs. His clientele came from both the North and South and from as far away as Europe seeking relaxation and restored health at his inn. Each evening, beautifully dressed ladies entered the dining room on the arms of wealthy gentlemen. Later, they enjoyed music and dancing. Men whose main interest was gambling were accommodated in a separate building. During the Civil War, the Confederate Army used Stribling Springs Inn as a hospital.[4]

Life at Stribling Springs exposed Francis Stribling to a

world far more cosmopolitan than the one that existed in most of Augusta County. Simply spending time at Stribling Springs and working in his father's law office probably helped the young Stribling acquire the organizational habits that would serve him well in his career as a physician.[5]

Stribling's father Erasmus died on July 3, 1858 at the home of his daughter, Mary Tate Lewis in Mason City, Virginia. His obituary in the Staunton Vindicator follows.

> Mr. Stribling was seventy-four years old. He had served in the Augusta County court and ran Stribling Springs Inn. For many years before his death he had suffered an adverse fortune. Erasmus Stribling was hospitable, sympathetic, well informed, and beloved by those who knew him. His house was a resort for the wealthy as well as a shelter for the distressed. Although dissipated and careless in his youth concerning religion, several years before his death, Stribling became an exemplary and worthy member of his church. When he could not attend the church, Stribling held services at home. By the time Erasmus Stribling died, most of his children had left the area. The elder Stribling was born at "Hopewell" on June 1, 1784. He studied at Washington College in 1800-1803 and became a lawyer and merchant. Stribling married Matilda Kinney in Staunton on April 23, 1807.[6]

Stribling was very devoted to family, especially his father. When he experienced financial trouble, the court appointed Chelsea Kinney, Erasmus Stribling's nephew, to land at Augusta Springs that Erasmus Stribling had owned since 1816. On October 1, 1843, Stribling purchased the land at auction for $2,300.[7] Four years later, he subdivided a fifty-acre parcel that contained his father's home place and gave his father a clear title to it.[8]

Stribling first studied under a physician in Staunton before beginning his formal medical training. He enrolled in the 1829-1830 session of the recently established medical school of the University of Virginia at Charlottesville, Va., and became its first graduate.[9] The medical school fell short of providing its students with the clinical experience they needed to practice medicine, however. It was particularly difficult for medical students to procure cadavers to dissect. It was said that under a blanket of darkness students sometimes snatched corpses of slaves from their graves.[10] Six students were given permission in 1831 to go to Prince George County on what was described as an "anatomical expedition."

In essence, Charlottesville's population could not support a clinic or hospital where medical students could observe various illnesses and practice surgery. The school finally decided that, until clinical facilities could be created, the university's medical students would have to gain their clinical experiences at other institutions.[11]

The university eventually rectified the limitations of its medical school by creating a first-year school of medicine superior to any existing in the nation at that time. Its nine-month sessions distinguished it from similar institutions in the North, where students participated in shorter sessions and were taught almost exclusively by lecture. Dr. Robley Dunglison, a professor of anatomy and medicine, later wrote, "One of the great advantages of the University of Virginia as a medical school for the first year (student) is that the student is not overburdened with lectures, and has time to study various subjects. This recommendation of the university's medical school, I frequently hear."[12] The university also did not allow its professors to engage in private practice, an activity that would perhaps distract them from their teaching duties.

In June of 1829, the University of Pennsylvania agreed to accept Virginia's graduates on an equal standing with their own students. Later, Professor Conrad of the University of Pennsylvania, wrote to Dr. Alfred Magill that, "the University of Virginia stands in high estimate, and the students of one year from your University almost invariably graduate in Philadelphia the second year at the head of their classes, being much better prepared in science than if they had attended their first year at Philadelphia."[13]

Stribling transferred to the University of Pennsylvania's medical school to attend its 1830-1831 session. The roots of the school went back to 1740. The medical school had grown because of the excellent reputations of the physicians who taught there. From 1800 until 1839, nearly 2,000 physicians graduated. Another 3,000, who attended for one year, went on to practice medicine without state licenses, a practice that was perfectly acceptable at the time.[14]

Stribling's graduation cards from the University of Pennsylvania described the curricula for its second-year medical students. A card from W.G. Horner, dean of the college, stated, "Mr. Francis F. Stribling of Virginia has matriculated in the Medical Department for the Sessions 1831." He received similar cards for each of the courses he completed in materia medica, chemistry, institutes and practice of medicine, clinical practice, principles and practice of surgery and diseases, anatomy, and principles of practice of surgery. Stribling's internship at the Philadelphia Almshouse allowed him to examine patients and prescribe remedies to cure them.[15]

After receiving his medical degree, Stribling returned to Staunton to practice medicine. He married Henrietta Cuthbert of Norfolk on May 17, 1832, with the Reverend Ebenezer Boyden of the Episcopal Church officiating. (16) Their marriage produced four children: Ella Matilda born in1833; Fannie Cuthbert in 1836; Francis, Jr. in 1845; and Henrietta Berkely in 1852.[17]

Later Stribling would be described as a kind indulgent father and a solicitous, loving husband. Although he suffered serious incidents of illness and his wife's health problems were on going, they were loving parents who created a warm home for their children. Furthermore, there was constant interaction between Stribling's children and their relatives in the area and those who lived elsewhere. The entire family also would have engaged in the religious and social activities of their church.

Stribling established a private medical practice in Staunton but did not make his mark in the general practice of medicine. His greatest contribution was as an advocate for the insane through the practice of moral medicine. As a result, Stribling would leave a lasting impact on the treatment of the insane in Virginia and elsewhere.

Concern for the insane can be identified prior to the American Revolution. The Virginia House of Burgesses passed An Act to Provide for the Support and Maintenance of Idiots, Lunatics and Other Persons of Unsound Minds in 1770. That effort had been strongly supported for years by former governor Francis Fauquier, and reflected a growing concern about the treatment of the insane in the Virginia colony. Part of its preamble stated:

> Whereas several persons of insane and disordered minds have been frequently wandering in different parts of this colony and no certain provision having

> been yet made either towards effecting a cure of those
> whose cases are not become quite, desperate, nor for
> restraining others who may be dangerous to society.[18]

As a result of the law, Eastern State Lunatic Asylum, located in Williamsburg, Virginia, was established. It admitted its first patients on October 12, 1773.

The Burgesses specified that the hospital admit only people who were either curable or dangerous. Indigents and nonviolent chronically insane persons were to be admitted, treated, cured and eventually discharged.[19] Patients were accepted regardless of their color, class, or ability to pay; slaves were the exception. For almost fifty years, Eastern Lunatic Asylum was the only institution for the insane in the nation administered and supported by a state.

Prior to the establishment of Eastern State, care of the indigent, the insane, beggars, vagrants, handicapped persons, and others unable to care for themselves, came under the authority of local officials or the established church. This often meant that families or other community members were given monetary subsidies to keep and maintain the insane at home. Others were placed in poorhouses or almshouses. At times they were even jailed.[20]

The Pennsylvania Hospital, founded by Philadelphia Quakers with the support of the colonial government in 1751, contained a separate ward to accommodate insane patients. Middle class lay reformers in New York pressured their colonial government for the establishment of psychiatric wards in their general hospitals.[21] As a totally state-supported institution Eastern State Hospital, however, represented a significant departure from those private efforts.

Although there are no statistics from this period that

indicate a rise in the number of insane, poverty and crime clearly were on the rise. In America's new industrial and urban society, these problems became even more apparent. Reform efforts to combat these "evils" began to take shape in the 1820s with the establishment of asylums that would at the same time alleviate the suffering of the insane and improve society.[22]

The causes of mental illness had long perplexed society. For centuries, poverty, crime, and mental illness were each seen as permanent social circumstances ordained by God as a test of Christian charity. Beginning in the sixteenth century, during what is now called the Age of Discovery, doctors began to adopt the view that insanity was a complex disease. Enlightenment philosophers Levinus Lemnius and Paracelus postulated that man was a product of his "total biological functions" and suggested that the insane had no control over their condition. Johann Weyer, the first scientist to concentrate exclusively on mental illness and thus the founder of modern psychiatry, advocated humanitarian treatment for the insane. His influence spread across Europe.

One of the first physicians to practice humanitarianism was France's Philippe Pinel. Pinel, the recognized founder of Moral Treatment, advocated kindness and limited the use of restraints when treating the mentally ill. In England, during the 18th—century, William Tuke recommended more benign treatment for the patients at his York Retreat, believing that it would allow the expression of their inborn goodness. During that same time, Italy's Vincenzo Chiarugi further suggested that a closer relationship between doctor and patient would bear good results in the treatment of the insane. Moral medicine crossed the Atlantic during the 18th—century when

Doctors Benjamin Rush and Eli Todd, while attending school in England, learned of the work being done for the insane. They incorporated variations of moral medicine into their own practices when they returned to the United States.[23]

> Moral medicine as a treatment for the insane dramatically changed not only the assumptions about insanity but eventually psychiatric practices in the treatment of the insane in the United States. It influenced superintendents of the New York Hospital, where a psychiatric department was founded in 1791. A number of other hospitals treating the insane opened in short order: Friends Hospital of Frankfort, Pennsylvania in 1819; The Hartford Retreat in 1824; and Bloomingdale Hospital in 1828.[24]

An act of the Virginia Legislature passed on January 22, 1825 created Western State Hospital. Not only had Eastern State Hospital outgrown its capacity, but transporting insane persons to Williamsburg from the western part of Virginia, which then included all of present-day West Virginia, was extremely difficult. Western State's location was ideal. It was located at the outskirts of Staunton, the Shenandoah Valley's largest town at the crossroad of two major roads. Built in the popular Greek Revival style, the hospital buildings were unsurpassed in the nation for their architectural beauty and function. Ample space, adequate ventilation, and regulation of light and heat, combined with the beauty of the Valley and surrounding mountains, were certain to have a positive effect on the lives and mental health of its patients.[25]

A court of directors, appointed by the state legislature to govern the hospital, soon selected Samuel M. Woodward as keeper, his wife Mary as matron and Doctor William Boys as the institution's first physician. Boys had received his education in Edinburgh, Scotland, and had lived in Philadelphia before moving to Staunton, where he became a prominent physician.

Western State's directors advertised the hospital's opening in a Richmond newspaper and subsequently sent copies of the advertisement to every county and corporation court in the Commonwealth. Its first patients who were males, arrived on July 24, 1828. One of them, twenty-eight-year-old schoolteacher Anderson Kendal from Orange, Virginia, suffered from an illness caused by excessive study. Robert Hunter, the other male patient, was a twenty-one-year-old farmer who was said to be insane over religion. Two female patients were admitted the next day. One, Catherine Smith, suffered from religious excitement.[26]

Applications soon overwhelmed the hospital. In response, its directors passed a resolution to admit only those patients who were violent enough to be dangerous to society, whose indecency offended society's moral sense, or whose reason might be restored.[27] Initially, the race of a prospective patient did not play a role in admission. Later, Stribling wrote Dorothea Dix that the hospital never admitted blacks although confusion on that issue surfaced later.[28]

The construction of Western State created excitement in the Staunton area. Stribling, who was seventeen years old at the time, probably watched the walls of Western State go up. He surely also knew when the first patients were admitted shortly before he left the area to attend the University of Virginia. Later, as a young doctor practicing medicine in Staunton, he undoubtedly was familiar with the hospital's medical practices and treatment of the insane by Boys.

Positions at Western State Lunatic Asylum attracted

qualified people for a number of reasons, not the least of which was the financial security of an annual salary. It is probable that Dr. Boys, Western State's first physician, was not surprised when Dr. Francis T. Stribling challenged him when his contract expired in early 1836. Stribling's education, established medical practice in Staunton, and influential family and social connections allowed him to replace Boys as physician on July 1, 1836 when he was only twenty-six years old. When Stribling became superintendent, the hospital had forty-four patients, twenty-five men and nineteen women. Some had been there since it opened in 1828. It had treated only 79 patients between then and when Stribling became superintendent.[29].

CHAPTER 2

A Bold New Physician

While Stribling may have had some exposure to moral medicine while he was a studying medicine in Philadelphia, he understood his lack of experience in administering his hospital or treating his newly acquired patients. Consequently, soon after his appointment, he visited mental hospitals in the middle and northern states. While there he established personal relationships with well-known doctors such as Luther Bell of Boston, Thomas Kirkbridge of Philadelphia, and others. Most important was that he learned that some of the insane could be cured if their disease was treated early and did not stem from some biological causes.[1]

Armed with knowledge from these doctors, Stribling returned to Western State with a bold new plan to change the way Virginia treated its insane. He understood that his plan would succeed only if existing policies at Western State were replaced with new ones. First, however, he had to educate his hospital's directors, the state's legislators, and the general public as to the nature of insanity and the importance of early treatment for the afflicted. Stribling concentrated first on his directors, since they held the keys to the funding that he would need from the legislature to incorporate the tenets of moral medicine into his practice.

Stribling used his first report to his directors to describe his overall goals in detail and the actions and funds that would be needed to implement them. He first acknowledged that, while Virginia had treated its insane with mildness and humanity in the past, Western State had become little more than a well-kept prison. It kept its occupants safe but failed to restore their sanity. "It should be mortifying," he wrote, "to the pride of every Virginian that the number of cures effected in her hospitals was trifling indeed when compared to those produced in hospitals in other parts of the Union."[2]

According to Stribling, those responsible for the insane had lost sight entirely of the means essential to restore the mental health of patients so that they could care for themselves. To achieve this goal, Stribling knew that the directors must discard their mistaken idea of economy and follow the example set by those managing similar institutions in other states. If they did not, Stribling challenged, Virginia's asylums would remain insignificant and obscure by comparison to other similar institutions. [3]

Stribling requested that his directors purchase more land, construct more buildings, change Western State's admission policy, and increase the number of attendants. He explained to them that patients could not be cured as long as they were confined without means of mental and physical exercise. Stribling also insisted that those who worked recovered sooner than those who did not work, as they had less time to concentrate on their delusions. Stribling's directors must have been stunned that the young doctor they had hired only six months earlier censured not only them and their contemporaries at Eastern State, but the entire Virginia legislature as well.

Stribling demonstrated his political acumen in his first report to the hospital's directors. He employed a pattern in that report that he would continue to use effectively for years. First, Stribling complimented his directors, then he described a problem, recommended a solution, and, requested additional funds to cover his proposals. The emotional imagery he employed shamed his directors, the legislature, and others into action. He also reveals his enthusiasm and impatience to get on with his work. Stribling's supreme self-confidence allowed him latitude to make negative statements that could have jeopardized his recent appointment. Stribling concluded his report by writing that he "wanted to discuss other topics, but would desist at present in order not to exhaust his directors' patience or present too many subjects to them at one time."[4]

After less than a year in his new position, Stribling had established an excellent relationship with his directors. He had cured some patients and submitted concrete plans to cure others. In their 1837 report to the legislature, the directors wrote that:

> They had witnessed with the liveliest satisfaction the zealous and indefatigable efforts of their able and accomplished physician, and those of his officers and employees. The most astonishing instances of cures had been effected within a few brief months. Patients who when received, were emaciated by disease and destitute of every ray of intellect, had been discharged in short time, restored both in body and mind. Experience confirmed that three-fourths of those

patients could have been cured if treatment had begun within a year after they became ill. [5]

The directors expressed their continued confidence in Stribling's system of moral treatment in preference to the antiquated practice of violence and coercion. In response to his requests, they purchased four acres of meadowland and fifty-six acres of upland adjacent to the hospital. They also provided the hospital with a piano, books, newspapers, and horse and carriage.

Western State's directors soon began to attach Stribling's annual reports to the ones that they submitted to the legislature. Stribling, who always took advantage of every opportunity, now had direct access to the members of the state legislature, and he used it to emphasize Western State's accomplishments. Throughout his career Stribling would use every opportunity to become more proficient in his profession. He was also an educator and understood that the better the legislature understood insanity and how to cure patients, the more likely they would be to fund his projects. It would not escape the legislature's notice that some of the innovations Stribling was suggesting would significantly decrease his hospital's expenses.

To that end, Stribling described how he cured patients and his statements are summarized below:

> His treatments included medical (appendix C) and moral means based on philosophy and physiology. Depending on circumstances, he used one or the other, but more often a blend of the two. Stribling found that patients whose brains had become abnormally affected only responded to medical means, while moral means alone cured some chronic patients. He defined moral means as everything other than

medical that could be brought to bear, directly or indirectly, upon the thoughts, feelings, passions, and propensities of the human mind and heart. [6]

The tenets of moral medicine included early treatment, occupation, classification, religion, diet, amusements, reduced use of restraints, and the removal of activities that aroused a patient's anger or passions. [7]

Stribling's contributions to moral medicine were described by Dr. Wyndham in his book, *Medicine in Virginia in the Nineteenth Century*:

> He was one of the first psychiatrists in this country to grasp the possibilities of humane treatment of the insane. By supplying occupation and amusement to the sufferers, and minimizing the circumstances productive of anger and passion, Stribling offered a great inducement to proper behavior and self-control. He also originated the system of furloughs now universally adopted by institutions of this character. [8]

Stribling accomplished many of his goals during his tenure even though he and other members of his family had been plagued with health problems since early in his career and they only worsened over the years. Mrs. Henrietta Stribling's health became so fragile in the 1850s that she often could not leave her room, and eventually she would become an invalid. [9] In 1850, Stribling and his family frequented a healing "springs" twelve miles from Staunton, recuperating from their ill health. [10] It worried his parents that their son Frank suffered from a weak constitution and poor vision. [11]

Stribling was so ill in August of 1852 that he could not respond to letters from Dix. When he felt better, Stribling wrote Dix that his illness, while not serious in nature, had caused him a great deal of pain. Stribling still had not completely recovered by the fall when he wrote to his directors that he anticipated he would have to resign at the end of another year. He continued that he felt confident that he had energetically promoted Western State for more than seven years. His directors were convinced that Stribling's exhausting labors and anxieties had caused his illness. They hoped that timely relaxation and exercise might restore his health. Indeed, Stribling's health must have improved because he remained at the hospital.[12]

Just four years later Stribling became so ill that he wrote his directors that he was resigning. It was in this letter that he would address overcrowding at his hospital. Stribling took the opportunity to reflect on his tenure on the hospital and his tenure there. When he became chief physician in 1836, the hospital had thirty-two patients, and now there were nearly 400, making Western State one of the largest hospitals for the insane in the United States.[13]

CHAPTER 3

Stribling Changes Practices, Policies, and Laws

S tribling soon changed many practices and procedures, and created new ones. Understanding that members of the state legislature were very busy, he increased the readability and validity of his reports by employing techniques that were ahead of their time. His new format contained easy-to-read tables that highlighted data on Western State that made it easier to compare his institution to similar ones elsewhere. For example, Stribling used one such report to convince the legislature to enlarge the state's two mental hospitals. Within it, he compared Virginia to New Hampshire, with its aggregate population of 280,000 and an insane population of 600; Connecticut with 298,000 and 700; Massachusetts with 612,000 and 1,000; and New York with 2,000,000 and 1,500. Based on that data and the capacity of its own two hospitals, Virginia, with a total population of at least 1,200,000, could expect to have from 600 to 800 untreated insane persons in the very near future.[1]

Well-trained employees were essential to Stribling's goal to create an orderly environment in his hospital. His employees should know exactly where they should be each hour of the day and what they should be doing. Such routines would also benefit the patients. Therefore, Stribling described their duties in great detail and placed them in a "regulation" book. In the future, as necessary, Stribling would create new regulations and revise existing ones. Because he believed that his attendant was the most important person in a patient's life, Stribling spent a great deal of time listing their duties that are described in Chapter 4. Regulations for some of the other employees are summarized in Appendix A. The regulations remain relevant, because they present an insight into the daily life of all of those at the hospital: staff, supervisory and other employees, patients, and servants.

Soon Stribling took other actions to improve the daily lives of his patients that did not require immediate additional funding. He understood that they were very sensitive in ways that were not always obvious; for example, even the clothes that they wore could adversely affect them. Under Virginia law, patients at Western State had been forced to wear coarse, uniform-type clothing that suggested to some of them that they were prisoners. Stribling realized that the uniforms dehumanized the patients and hindered their recovery. Therefore, in 1838, he suggested that the law be modified to provide them with clothes similar to what they had worn before entering the hospital.[2]

Since warm baths soothed patients, thus helping them to recover, Stribling suggested that they be built.[3] Although he did not want to appear extravagant, Stribling also asked his directors to purchase a neat, two-horse carriage that could be used to exercise convalescents and invalids. The motion the carriage produced operated directly on the patient's mind through the medium of his senses, creating emotions of both pride and pleasure.[4]

An important new practice was to separate patients who earlier had been thrown together indiscriminately. Thus, chaos was eliminated when Stribling separated them according to the severity of their insanity: convalescent patients from those who were incurable; the wealthy, educated, and refined from those supported by the state; and noisy and violent ones from those who were quiet and tranquil. There were exceptions. Stribling placed educated individuals accustomed to good society with first-class patients, even if they were maintained at state expense. And he placed any paying patient, whose conduct distracted others, with wards of the state with similar dispositions and habits.[5]

Later on Stribling requested funds to construct two small buildings remote from the others, one for females and the other for males. Both would be used exclusively for noisy and raving maniacs "whose noise sometimes disturbed the establishment, and retarded the recovery of other patients."[6] Several benefits resulted from classification. Many patients strove to be promoted to a higher class because they valued the good opinion of their fellow men. The self-control and self-respect they needed to maintain or improve their position not only created a more cheerful atmosphere throughout the hospital, but also helped cure the patients.

In order to avoid some of the problems and pitfalls experienced by his fellow superintendents, Stribing often turned to them for advice. For example, excessive drinking by caretakers and patients had plagued many institutions. Therefore, he instructed his employees to keep all liquor in the barroom, whose only key was kept by the matron. She received and disbursed all liquor and recorded each transaction by date, type of liquor, quantity received or given out, and the recipient. The matron was to list any quantity, however small, even if she was sending it to the superintendent, steward, assistant physicians, attendants, servants, or only using it for culinary purposes.[7]

Stribling engaged in research and careful planning before he requested expenditures to improve Western State. An example of his attention to detail is shown in his instructions to his employee Blackburn before sending him to northern hospitals to gain information on similar equipment used by superintendents there. He was to visit two hospitals in Pennsylvania, one in New Jersey, New York City Hospital, and other public institutions that had similar systems. While there, he was to investigate ways to construct water closets, urinals, downward ventilation and tools to remove obstructions, protect floors, and prevent the lower story from being damaged by an overflow from an upper one. In addition, Blackburn was to examine bathing fixtures for hot or cold water and the number required for each floor of the hospital. During the same time, he was to review maintenance procedures; numbers of mechanics to operate the equipment, their wages, gas records and procedures. Moreover, Stribling wanted to know the price of a suitable generator for the kitchen, and also, Blackburn was given a list of items to purchase or exchange.[8]

For some time, Stribling and other superintendents had realized the need for a formal way to exchange information and improve personal relationships. An important first step occurred in 1844 when Dr. Samuel B. Woodward, the superintendent of the State Lunatic Hospital at Worcester, Massachusetts, visited Stribling at Western State. It may have been then when the two physicians conceived the idea of a nationwide association of medical superintendents. Wherever the idea was first conceived, thirteen superintendents led by Woodward and Stribling met in Philadelphia on October 16, 1844, when they established "The Association of Medical Superintendents of American Institutions for the Insane"(Superintendents' Association) that eventually evolved into "The American Psychiatric Association."[9]

Its members had an enormous influence on the treatment of the insane in the nation. The Association published the "American Journal of Insanity" with its members writing most of the articles. After that, their thoughts and experiences became more available to other association members, legislators, and lay persons throughout the nation. The dedication of the members was shown by their willingness to travel over bad roads where they sometimes experienced unpleasant weather in order to attend their annual meetings.

Stribling and his peers also benefited when the association published in their proceeding conversations of small groups of individual members who focused on a particular topic. They remain invaluable to those studying the evolution of the superintendents' practices in areas improving patient care.

Unfortunately, this story only could concentrate on a few articles important to the evolution of moral medicine, among them how the superintendents viewed insane women and blacks in the context of Stribling's times. The Superintendents Association eventually evolved into the American Psychiatric Association.

An article written by Dr. Edward Jarvis in 1831 entitled "On the Proposed Increased in Insanity" gave the early superintendents an historical context within which they could evaluate their own thoughts, practices and experiences.[10]

Certainly, his article emphasized the importance to physicians and others to understand facts versus thoughts so that misconceptions could be eliminated that might result in unfortunate treatments or policies. Jarvis is described briefly in the following abridgement.

> His importance lay precisely in his efforts to unify medicine, science, and religion; he insisted that disease could never be understood apart from individual behavior or the state of society. From this followed his statistical research on the social basis of insanity and his efforts to modernize the federal census. In many ways he anticipated the emergence of the social and behavioral sciences, and the belief that morbidity and mortality patterns were but a reflection of the social and physical environment.[11]

An abridgement of his article follows.

> It is impossible to demonstrate whether lunacy is increasing, stationary, or diminishing, in proportion to the advancement of the population, for want of definite and reliable facts. Nor can we show how many insane persons there are now, and still less show how many there have been at any previous period.[12]
> Many civilizations contained persons who became insane to gain advantage over others or for self-preservation. Engaging in those activities caused the mind to expend immense amounts of energy. The result was a person's mind being overpowered by anxiety that taxed his brain to where it sometimes faltered or acted with uncertainty.[13] Over time, the result could be insanity.[14]
> Many cases of insanity have been the same in all ages, in all nations, and in all states of barbarism and civilizations. Some persons become insane because they are filled with malignant and evil passions such as anger, hatred, jealously, pride and violent temper.

Such causes probably exist with varying amounts of influence on the sanity of the brain.[15]

Some simple men, who a century earlier, thought only about obtaining daily sustenance, now study subjects that compel their brains to labor with greater energy and exhausting zeal than those of any former generation. Results are students who grapple with subjects that they can not master and sink under the burden of perplexity that they could not unravel. Some intently study politics, state or national affairs, subjects of legislation, the banking system, tariffs, licenses, etc., or public moral questions such as slavery, temperance and general or specific reforms. Any or all of them can impose great anxiety and mental labors that often resulted in insanity.[16]

Accepting paying patients was suggested by Stribling to his directors in 1838. For some time, wealthy families throughout Virginia and some southern states had been sending their insane relatives to hospitals in the North because they provided accommodations that were more comfortable than those available at Eastern and Western State. It was probable that others had not wanted their relatives in an institution that contained indigent persons.

Stribling strove to change that image of Western State by persuading his directors to obtain funds to make changes for the comfort of a limited number of paying patients. His directors acquiesced, and by 1841, thirty-four of them paid up to $213 a month for their care. By comparison, the state provided $88 for each pauper.[17] Stribling probably advertised in newspapers with notices similar to the one that Eastern State used later. As a consequence of those efforts, wealthy Virginians began to transfer their insane relatives to Western State from the hospitals in Philadelphia, Pennsylvania, and Hartford, Connecticut to Western State.[18]

Stribling understood that it was important to change the public's negative attitudes toward hospitals for the insane that caused some families to question the care their insane relative might receive in one of them. Even worse, some families were indifferent to or did not understand insanity, others were ashamed to have an insane relative, or feared the expense of hospitalization. Consequently, many families postponed seeking help for an insane relative, hindering his cure.

To counter those views and other prevailing attitudes of the day, Stribling appealed to the public's sense of Christian charity. He believed that it was often counterproductive to keep an insane person at home. Factors there sometimes contributed to the onset of mental illness, and well-meaning family members often were incapable of actually treating their relative. Frequently, an individual who began to exhibit signs of insanity no longer interacted with family and friends in a normal manner. He often distorted the actions of anyone who attempted to help him and rejected family members whom he sometimes associated with his illness. The common practice of restraining or isolating the insane person made a cure more elusive.

Further, it was more difficult for physicians to treat an insane person at home. All too often, a physician and the patient's family could become convinced too quickly that their relative could not be helped, and consequently, stop searching for a cure.[19] Stribling also believed that sometimes an insane person's chances of improving only with a change of scenery, or new associations with people who were kind and treated him with respect. In the event, however, that a patient suffered from an unrelated serious physical illness that made travel too difficult or dangerous for him to travel, he should remain at home. Overall, most of the insane should be in hospitals.[20]

During its 1840-41 the House of Delegates formed a committee to suggest ways to revise the basic text of the Virginia law concerning admissions. Since the committee felt incompetent to deal intelligently with the subject, they enlisted Stribling and Dr. Galt of Eastern State, along with a member from each of their respective court of directors, to assist them. Instead of suggesting changes, Stribling took the opportunity to rewrite the entire bill and present it to committee. The committee subsequently reported the bill to the legislature without material amendment. The new law passed and Stribling was credited as its author.[21]

The revised law established a new governing authority and policy for every individual or institution in the state that cared for the insane. Under the new law, the governor instead of the directors selected superintendents who could not live more than twelve miles from their hospital. The superintendent, officers, and attendants of the hospital were exempt from serving on juries, working on public roads, or performing military duty in time of peace.

The revised law described how to determine insanity and the procedures to be followed for those who needed to be hospitalized. It required that three justices determined a person's insanity by using a more complex process. The justices summoned those who knew the alleged insane person as well as his physician, if he had one. The following questions would aid the justices in their determination:

> What was the person's age and marital status?
> If married, how many children did he or she have?
> What were his or her habits and circumstances?

When had indications of the person's derangement first appeared?

Was the disease increasing, declining, or stationary?

Were there periodical improvements or rational intervals?

If the person was violent, how long had he been so?

Did the person's deranged mind concentrate on various subjects or only one?

What did friends and neighbors believe caused his derangement?

Had the person experienced earlier attacks?

What changes had occurred in bodily conditions since the person's last attack?

Had the person shown any disposition to injure himself or others?

Had any restraint or confinement been imposed?

Had any of the person's relatives been insane?

Did he or she have a history of bodily diseases such as suppression of excretory passages, eruptions, sores, injuries, and etc.?

Had curative means been pursued to cure and to what effect?

Had bloodletting, cathartics, low diet, etc. been resorted to, and to what extent?

If two of the three justices agreed that the person was insane, they authorized his removal to the nearest hospital for the insane. If that hospital did not have a vacancy, the patient was sent to Virginia's other hospital for the insane. The justices provided the results of their inquiry concerning the prospective patient to the hospital's superintendent, who placed them before his directors. By examining the evidence and the patient, the directors made the final determination to either admit or discharge the applicant.

If an insane person confined in a hospital or a prison was restored to sanity, the directors or specified court officials were to discharge him and give him a certificate verifying his cure. They also could deliver an insane person to any friend who gave bond and security for him. An estate that provided a patient with an income was required to pay for his care. The law also contained many procedures describing how the estate of an insane person must be handled.[22]

In 1836 Stribling had described the difference between idiocy and dementia. An idiot was one "who at an early age, the application of physical causes operated to oppose the development of the cerebral organs. Consequently, the intellect was prevented from manifesting itself." In those suffering dementia, the brain had sufficiently developed and at one time had performed its intellectual functions until due to some moral or physical cause, or both, "those functions simply had not been perverted or deranged, but paralyzed and destroyed."[23]

Once a family decided to place an insane relative in an institution, it often deceived him in order to get him there. Stribling strongly disapproved of such actions because it generated a strong resentment from the patient and increased the likelihood that he might attempt to escape. He insisted that the person committing an insane person make it clear to him where he was going and why. Then if the person violently resisted and force was required, it was at least force without deception. Stribling wanted to avoid compounding the individual's mental problems with duplicity.[24]

Stribling believed that the first impression that a new patient had of the hospital was of the utmost importance. He probably had been traumatized when he was removed from his previous environment. Even if it had been unpleasant, it was known to him. And one of the patients' greatest fears was of the unknown. It was only natural, therefore, that an insane patient often would suspect his new caretaker's good intention.

It was important, therefore that the physician, officers, and other caretakers treat him kindly, thus setting the stage for his cure. Stribling insisted that from the time the physical was taking place and afterwards, the caretakers avoid any deception, keep every promise, and extend every friendship to the patient. It was also an excellent time for the physician to convince his patient that the physician strongly believed in his own prescriptions. A patient, Stribling thought, was more likely to accept firm decisions made by the staff if he understood that his physician would do what was necessary to implement them.[25]

Most applicants to Western State were admitted without a medical history. Most were unable to describe their prior condition; and some of their relatives, who could provide information, often were not forthcoming. Consequently, Stribling's initial examination of a new patient was critical. He first determined whether or not the patient's problem was the result of or aggravated by a brain condition that was connected to a diseased organ. If the brain seemed affected, Stribling attempted to locate the exact area of cerebral damage. While he did not consider the mind as a mere function of the brain, Stribling belonged to that class of mental pathologists who viewed all its abnormal manifestations as resulting from some idiopathic or sympathetic affection of this organ.

Stribling also looked for symptoms that might indicate insanity. He first examined the patient's temperament, previous habits, and disposition; and finally, the circumstances under which the symptoms had developed. He recorded his observations of the person during the interview, such as his facial expression and manner.[26]

Stribling had earlier observed that nearly all of the insane fell under the definition of monomania or partial insanity, mania or dementia, melancholia or hypochondriasis, and idiocy. Others were insane because of physical causes such as blows to the head, suppression of bowels, and fever. Still others suffered inherited conditions such as epilepsy, and debility of the nervous system. Intemperance at that time was viewed as insanity. Moral causes included domestic grief, excess study, reversal of fortune, jealousy, hopeless love, unhappy marriage, harsh treatment, and fanaticism.[27]

CHAPTER 4

Activities at Western State

A visitor to Western State a few years after Stribling became superintendent, would have seen patients, with their attendants by their side, engaging in a variety of activities, inside and outside the hospital. Slave servants would be working throughout the buildings. Dr. Stribling may have been visiting patients or in his office, attending to a variety of administrative tasks. His staff would be overseeing hospital employees and assuring that they were following procedures. A memorial to Stribling in 1874 best describes his successful administration of his hospital.

> Under Stribling's hand, everything had been so perfect in its working that, even though he was no longer there, the hundred of patients, officers, and attendants were moving with the regularity of clock-work.[1]

Stribling believed that an attendant was the most important person in a patient's life, and the one most able to effect his cure. Therefore, he spent a great deal of time selecting and training attendants in the art of therapeutic relationships. The order provided by the attendants's presence reassured his patients and allowed more freedom for them. He should strive to become his patient's "companion" and "sympathizing friend" because having a friend was especially important to the patient.

Attendants were responsible for the health and safety of their charges. Each morning, the attendant assured that his patients were properly washed, their hair combed, and that they were decently dressed for the day. He attended them at meals to ensure that they received their proper supply of food and fed those who could not feed themselves. He insured that patients did not carry utensils away from the table or have access to a razor, knife, or any dangerous weapon or instrument without permission of an officer.

Each attendant was to respect his patients' privacy by not commenting publicly on their conduct or conversations. He must never ridicule, mock, or hurt a patient's feelings. Instead, Stribling advised attendants to show affection, speak to their patients in a mild and gentle tone, soothe and calm them when they were irritated, and encourage them when they were melancholy or depressed.

The attendant must maintain his own authority by his deportment. Even when one of his patients was unsettled and abusive, the attendant must remain calm and not recriminate, scold, irritate, or dictate to him unless it was absolutely necessary. The attendant, however, must stop any improper conversations or altercations between patients, but in the gentlest manner. An attendant, however, had to be sure other patients and employees were not disturbed. An attendant must never lay violent hands on a patient except in self-defense or to prevent the patient from injuring himself or others. Only an officer could authorize the use of restraints such as muffs, mittens or wristbands on patients.

The attendant also was responsible to keep his patients safe in other ways. He was to assure that doors were locked, fires banked, and lamps checked. He relinquished his keys only to an officer unless the physician had ordered him otherwise. He was not to admit anyone into the patients' apartments without the physician's permission. An attendant was expected to show great respect and attention to hospital visitors.

Only officers had the authority to give an attendant permission to leave the hospital, and when he left, he had to return by 9 p.m., unless the officer gave him permission to stay out longer. An attendant had to give the hospital at least fifteen days' notice prior to resignation. However, at a time when labor was cheap and expendable, Stribling took every opportunity to publicly commend the hospital's attendants and other employees for the high quality of their work.[2]

Stribling continued to seek funds to cure more patients by practicing more of the tenets of moral medicine. They included occupation, diet, amusements, and religion. A high priority was occupation because patients who worked had less time to concentrate on their delusions. Earlier Stribling had convinced his directors of its importance by asking his friend Dr. Luther Bell to describe how he had used occupation to cure his patients. Bell first reported how men who had not worked for some time often entered his hospital prostrate, with their joints flexed and stiffened, and their feet and legs swollen and ulcerated. Bell first placed them on a regular diet and medicated them when necessary before leading them into the habits of labor.

Bell's plan required a smaller attendant-to-patient ratio because such treatment required more attendants who could exercise considerable perseverance and patience. One attendant could work only with only four or five such patients at a time, however, as his patients improved, he could oversee between six and eight. Bell observed that patients who worked were easier to manage because they gradually became less excitable and slept better. His attendants confirmed that once a new patient began working, he soon got well. Even professional men such as merchants, clerks and others, who had never engaged in physical work, grew to appreciate the virtue of labor.[3]

Stribling offered a personal example of how he had combined amusement and occupation to cure one of his patients. The patient had been hospitalized for nine years, a victim of furious madness and extreme violence. Although he enjoyed some intervals of calm, the simple appearance of a preacher or mere mention of his wife would instantly transform him into a madman. Stribling did not believe that medicine would help this patient, but he observed that the patient seemed interested in games. Stribling gave him a backgammon board, a pack of cards, a set of quoits, and a number of marbles. Soon the patient and some of his fellow patients were nearly constantly involved with one or another of the games. After about eight months, the patient voluntarily began cane making and soon was making money. Not long afterward, Stribling recommend that he be discharged.[4]

In 1841, Stribling reported to the directors his many accomplishments over the five years he had been Western State's physician. An important goal had been to create an environment that was as similar as possible to the one that the patients had experienced before they entered the hospital. For example, a healthy diet that was as similar as possible to what they had at home, work, and participation in religious and leisure activities.

As to occupation, Stribling and his officers did not force a patient to work at a job to which he objected, but he could not remain idle. Male patients could cultivate the land and raise food for the hospital. Stribling further suggested that, rather than purchasing clothes for the patients, the hospital purchase material and allow female patients to make them. Such activities helped cure the patients and created economic benefits for the hospital because it would not have to pay others for work that the patients could do.[5]

Occupation had proved especially beneficial to his patients. Fifty-one of the 73 males were working. They cultivated the farm and gardens, cut wood, constructed fences, and took care of the stock. They also worked in the orchard that contained about 150 grafted apple trees, together with plum, pear, cherry, and peach trees. The vegetables and fruits the patients produced supplied the hospital during the summer, and provided some surplus to store for the fall and winter.[6]

Stribling encouraged men who were too weak to work to form a pseudo-militia company complete with badges that designated rank. Some of the men who had been indifferent to other forms of work or amusement responded favorably to marching and the requirements of dress and order. When formation took place, they paraded to the tap of a drum. They often marched for miles under the supervision of an attendant. The militia was a success and continued until its captain was discharged from the hospital.[7]

Thirty-five of the forty-nine women patients were working in appropriate jobs. For various reasons, the rest were idle. Some of the women who could have worked in the kitchen or laundry refused to work with slaves, and Stribling did not feel at liberty to overrule their opposition or force the issue. Others created fine needlework that was greatly admired. A sewing group called the "Chapel Society" attracted patients who previously had been unwilling to sew. They sold their fancywork outside the institution. Other women made dresses, shifts, pantaloons, aprons, vests, shirts, bonnets, and caps. They also knitted stockings and socks; hemmed handkerchiefs; and made a variety of other products such as suspenders, comforts, quilts, bedspreads, sheets, bed ticks, bolster and pillow ticks, tablecloths, towels, and curtains. In addition, they cut yarn, spun, double—twisted, and sewed carpet rags. The female patients also mended and darned clothes for patients and servants, thereby repairing clothing that would have otherwise been discarded.[8]

Nearly all the work that occupied the patients at the hospital was similar to that they engaged in before they became ill, and what they might return to after they were released. Stribling described every article that the patients produced and included them in his reports to his directors. He wanted to assure that economic benefits to the hospital because of patient labor were evident to the legislature. Over the next years, Stribling continued to seek funds to increase the quantity and variety of jobs. By 1846, he sought funds for a new, two-story brick building that would be used by the master mechanic, carpenters, cabinetmakers, and those making hats, mattresses, brooms, mats, and storage room. [9]

For patients unaccustomed to labor, Stribling requested that the directors purchase a variety of items that allowed them to engage in constructive activities. Subsequently, a billiard table, ninepin bowling, chess, checkers, and other games, and musical instruments were added to the hospital's collection. Stribling wrote that, "soon the tones of a well-strung piano, the soothing melody of the flute, and the enlivening notes of the violin, produced by a skillful performer, tranquilized the furious and animated and cheered those who were sometimes sad and gloomy."[10]

Stribling encouraged other activities for all patients who could participate in them. Unaccompanied, except by each other, patients walked to town, attended church, called on acquaintances, listened to legal and published debates, and frequented places of amusement, provided that they did not cause any disturbance of the peace, violate good order, or breach decorum. Stribling believed that this freedom was instrumental in restoring their bodies and minds. Other patients wrote letters to friends and essays on scientific, literary and political subjects. A debating society was partially organized and a mock court established, both of which interested patients and benefited them.[11]

Since reading itself was treatment, Stribling urgently requested a library to provide books for those with less severe afflictions, especially those with hypochondria. Because the *Staunton Spectator* gave the hospital complimentary newspapers, Stribling asked other editors to do the same. He stated that, "if editors could see how happy the papers made the patients, they would believe that it was more blessed to give than to receive. Even when the news was old, patients still expressed pleasure in reading it. They were most happy in possessing their local newspapers. Women especially enjoyed religious topics."[12]

Stribling took obvious pleasure in the patients' activities. He wrote that often, as he walked through the wards of his hospital, he enjoyed listening to the music from the piano, guitars, and other instruments. It pleased him to pass through a corridor where he could see a female patient skillfully manipulating an old-fashioned spinning wheel.[13]

Stribling believed that proper food affected his patients' health, and nourishment should do more than satisfy the patients' need for sustenance. They were more contented when they received food similar to what they had eaten at home. Stribling created a monthly menu that contained wholesome and nutritious food for each class of patients, including wheat and corn bread, coffee, tea, milk, butter, bacon, beef, veal, mutton, poultry, and various fruits and vegetables that were abundant in the area. Stribling stressed, however, that he did not cater to his patients or give them luxuries.

In his 1839 annual report, Stribling wrote that he had begun to seat patients who were not violent or noisy at tables for meals. Some of them had not seen a table set for a meal for ten years, and others had not eaten at one for five years. This privilege, he maintained, caused patients to be more satisfied, thereby aiding their recovery. The day the new program was implemented was memorable. Amid the expected confusion as the patients were seated, Stribling described some of the actions of a patient known as Lord Primate.

> He knocked on the table, and displayed all of the gravity and sanctity that belonged to the religious life of which he imagined himself a member. In an authoritative tone, Lord Primate commanded order in an authoritative tone; and if by magic, everyone sprang to their feet and fastened their eyes upon him. Having their attention, he reminded the patients of

their relation to the Supreme Being, who had
graciously provided food for them. He chided those
who began to eat before a blessing was said. Then,
Lord Primate took from his pocket a long prayer,
seemingly one that he had written for the occasion,
and read it to the amazed but attentive group.[14]

The patients enjoyed eating in the dining room and were
denied the privilege only because of physical problems.

As early as 1836, Stribling had discovered that many of
his patients were interested in access to religious services.
Those who had active religious lives before they became ill
asked him to provide religious services at the hospital. A
summary of his decision on the issue follows. Stribling wasn't
sure if he should do so because some of his patients were ill
because of "religious excitement." Still, he researched
hospitals in both the United States and Europe, and
discovered that in their institutions, religion was one of the
least contributing causes of mental illness. Rather than
agitating patients, religion seemed to soothe their feelings,
awake their affections, and focus their minds on memories of
better days.

Stribling realized that many of his patients were strongly
attached to religion and most of them were perfectly capable
of moral instruction and responsibility. He further believed
that through some type of religious practices even delusional
patients might maintain a clear sense of right and wrong as
well as a concept of their relationship to God. Stribling
concluded that responsible patients deserved an opportunity
to participate in religious services and seek spiritual
improvement. He believed that even those who were not
interested in religion, would benefit from religious instruction

because it would provide a break in their monotonous routine.[15]

However, Stribling did not trust fanatical preachers who presented a Supreme Deity full of wrath and vengeance because he had no desire to promote terror and alarm in his patients. If they were to benefit from religion, he believed that it should be presented zealously, tenderly, affectionately and carefully to his patients existing between the extremes of violence and idiocy.[16]

Surprised and suspicious by Stribling's request to employ a chaplain, his directors refused. Undeterred, he assembled patients whom he believed would profit from some religious instruction each Sunday afternoon, read them a sermon, and led them in prayer. The directors eventually relented and granted Stribling funds to hire a minister.[17] As oversight, Stribling carefully reviewed the minister's sermons to ensure that they came from the Scripture but were not full of hellfire and damnation.

The hospital provided services daily and on Sunday mornings and afternoons when the hospital choir sang. Patients eagerly awaited the Sabbath and considered it the most enjoyable day of the week. They found the services so valuable that they exhibited an unusual degree of self-control, even those who otherwise lacked it, in order to participate. Patients chose their own seats and those who considered themselves divine placed themselves in the most prominent seats. "Lord Primate" sat before the group; the "Virgin Mary" sat to his right; the "Fallen Angel Appollyon" on the left; and the "Mother of the Ten Tribes of Israel" in front.

By the beginning of the 1840s about eighty percent of the patients attended religious services on a regular basis.[18]

Innovations such as religious instruction combined with the many others introduced by Stribling enhanced Western State's reputation with the public and politicians in Richmond.

In 1851, the citizens of Staunton, including Stribling and his employees, were thrilled when President Millard Fillmore and philanthropist W.W. Corcoran visited Staunton on their way to White Sulfur Springs. They spent the night in town and attended church in Western State's chapel the next morning. It was the first time either of them had witnessed insane persons gathered for worship. Corcoran, deeply impressed by the devout attention of the patients and their evident enjoyment of the service, later gave Western State a fine pipe organ valued at $1,000.[19] The organ was built by Henry Erben & Co., a firm that built many organs for Southern institutions.[20]

Nearly all of the patients at Western State would have been aware of serious diseases among themselves, and also probably would have been terrified of fire. Certainly, Stribling and all of his employees greatly feared both because of their own experiences. A major disaster at Western State had been barely averted in 1837 when a chimney fire was extinguished by the quick actions of hospital employees. It had been abundantly clear that the hospital required better access to water. The directors wrote the legislature that "they could scarcely conceive a more horrid scene than Western State being enveloped in flames, with seventy or eighty patients in excruciating pain confined in their cells by iron bars, and crying out for relief that no one watching could give them." [21]

In their annual report to the legislature, the directors requested funds to replace the institution's shingle roof with tin. If the improvements were not made "incidents similar to several that occurred in the past year could cause the destruction of Western State by fire, resulting in an enormous loss of public property and causing the inevitable death to a large number of the hospital's unfortunate inmates." [22]

Another serious fire would occur later in November of 1855. A small, detached building that housed sixteen disturbed female patients burned as a result of a chimney fire. In October of the following year, yet another fire destroyed a similar building occupied by male patients. Circumstantial evidence suggested that a patient obsessed with fire set the second fire. Stribling was certain that the culprit was inspired to act by the sight of the first fire, and he was concerned that other patients could be similarly influenced, increasing the possibility of another incident. As a result, Stribling instituted a program of fire drills and instruction in fire fighting. [23]

Stribling and his patients faced a different threat in 1847 when an epidemic of typhoid fever swept through the hospital. Approximately thirty staff members and patients contracted the dreaded disease and were ill from five to eight weeks. Two deaths resulted from the epidemic, those of a female patient and a servant. [24]

Fortunately, a similar disease would not occur until 1872. Neither Stribling nor his officers could have prevented an outbreak of small pox that could have caused an epidemic. The dreaded disease was so contagious that it struck fear in the hearts of those in charge of any institution with large numbers of people. Later when Stribling described the smallpox incident to his directors, he wrote that only immediate action by Western State's officers kept an epidemic from occurring.

The episode began in March of 1872 when a black male servant was granted a week's leave to visit Washington and Baltimore. When he returned to resume his duties he seemed well, therefore, it did not occur to the officers of the hospital to restrict the servant's contact with patients or caretakers. A few days later when he complained of physical discomfort, the doctors treated him for inflammation of his mucous membrane. On the ninth day after his return, the servant was diagnosed with small pox and isolated. Stribling and his officers immediately used disinfectants, vaccination and revaccination on all of their employees. The servant recovered and enjoyed good health, and fortunately, no other cases occurred in the area. Stribling believed that a Higher Power had protected the patients and employees at Western State and rescued them from a serious threat.[25]

An institution's policy on the use of restraints greatly affected the lives of its patients. Stribling wrote that when the general public had become aware of how hospital employees used restraints to control insane persons, they made their opposition known. He suggested that the public forget the inhumane treatment of patients in the past, since most hospitals no longer used those extreme practices.

Stribling believed that tender treatment invariably produced the best effect. Having someone to talk to often kept a patient from needing restraints. He trained his caretakers to listen carefully to everything a patient said and to convince him that he was believed. They were to persuade the patient they were his friends, interested in his welfare, health, and comfort. Because nearly all people were sensitive to being respected, when a patient began to take pride in himself, he placed more confidence in others.

While Stribling was never able to do away with restraints completely, he used them only as a last resort to keep a patient from harming himself or others. Even then, he did not allow any procedure that could be interpreted as coercion. When all else failed, caretakers could restrain a patient by placing long sleeves, mittens, and wristbands on him. If those did not work, they put the patient in a confining chair, and that usually produced positive effects. Eventually, caretakers reduced restraints to the muff, straight waistcoat, and chair. Stribling would immediately discharge any employee he found guilty of treating a patient in a rough manner.[26]

Other superintendents throughout the nation faced restraint problems similar to those discussed by Stribling. When a growing insane population overcrowded hospitals, without increased funding, many superintendents believed that they had no choice but to use more restraints. In 1859, Dr. J. J. McIlhenny addressed the use of restraints in a paper entitled "The Various Means of Restraints for the Violently Insane."[27] which led to an in-depth discussion among superintendents on the subject that is described in more detail in Appendix B.

Stribling understood that families remained concerned about their relatives that remained in his hospital. Letters that he wrote to them in the 1850s reveal how he dealt with them in a sympathetic, but realistic way. Those letters give us further insight into the lives of the patients.

Stribling wrote to Dr. Calloway on August 2, 1856, describing a patient named Massie. He was frank, communicative, intelligent, and courteous, and not as ill as Stribling had anticipated. Although his nervous system was disordered, his intellect appeared almost unimpaired. Massie's unfortunate behavior operating on his disordered nervous system could have produced his symptoms. Stribling prescribed medicine for Massie, and suggested that he shower every day, exercise in open air, attend to his business when possible, and visit neighbors and friends who were cheerful.[28]

When Stribling learned that the children of one of his patients were seriously ill, he wrote the patient's husband, Thomas Taylor, that his wife had improved and wanted to return home. Stribling thought that she was one of those patients who would be injured if she were detained too long in a hospital. Stribling worried, however, that should she return home to find her children ill, and was too fatigued to nurse them, she might regress. After carefully weighing her situation, he suggested that Taylor take her home, especially if either of the children was in danger.[29]

Another of Stribling's patients grew distressed because he believed that his former business partner might assassinate his character in a book that he was writing. Such an attack could destroy not only his reputation, but also that of his wife and their friends. The patient's distress was enough to cause Stribling to write to the partner and ask him to inform him candidly whether or not it was his intent to assail the patient's character.[30]

The constant and desperate attempts to escape by another patient caused Stribling to write to his mother, Mrs. Bowley, that her son had recently torn down the walls of his room, broken his bedstead, forced the bars at his window, and left no means untried in his attempts to escape. Stribling assured her that her son was still allowed outside to exercise under supervision, his health was reasonably good and his appetite ample. Stribling cautioned her that the patient would sleep better if he were not always on the watch for an opportunity to escape.[31]

Close family members of a patient named Mrs. Moffett were concerned about their mother, who was upset that she had agreed to allow her daughter (Mrs. Moffett) to be placed in the hospital. One son offered to pay his mother's board if Stribling would allow her to attend Mrs. Moffett at the hospital. Stribling replied that doing so was utterly impracticable and could counteract his efforts to help the patient. He also opposed the suggestion that the mother board in the neighborhood in order to see her daughter occasionally. Stribling wrote that such action would increase her daughter's restlessness, who insisted that she was in constant danger. Mrs. Moffett often refused to leave the building, yet once outside, she resisted going back in. Stribling suggested that her family move Mrs. Moffett to a place where she and her mother could be together.[32]

Stribling involved himself when he was concerned about patients with other problems. He wrote the mother of a patient named Anthony because he had not recovered from an attack of diarrhea that had seriously affected his health. Suggesting to Anthony that he might not live, Stribling tried to obtain his thoughts on death and eternity. Anthony responded only with wild laughing and showed no desire to see his parents.[33]

At the same time Stribling was writing to the families of

his patients, he also would have been involved in a large amount of correspondence with others. Three examples follow. A man named Chandler owed money to the hospital and also to the undertaker for expenses related to his brother's death. The undertaker was a poor man with a dependent family who needed the money owed him. Stribling offered to reimburse the undertaker if Chandler would send him a check.[34]

In another letter, Stribling reprimanded Samuel Woodward, his steward. Although Stribling permitted officers and attendants to invite visitors to breakfast or dinner at the hospital, it had come to his attention that Woodward was abusing the privilege. Stribling reminded him that the privilege lasted only if it did not cause a problem. He reminded Woodward that he knew that he could not give his visitors a private table and they had to eat the same food given to the patients. Stribling had noticed that Woodward was not abiding by the rules, although he knew them. [35]

On December 17, 1857, Stribling wrote Nathaniel Massie, a member of the legislative committee of lunatic asylums, requesting his prompt attention to Western State's serious financial problems. The hospital had begun the fiscal year without a dollar in its treasury, and presently was in debt $125.34. Consequently, there was no money to clothe, feed, and otherwise provide for the patients. The Valley Bank of Staunton had thus far accommodated them, but Stribling had no assurance of further aid. Indeed, he feared that he could not obtain it. He asked that Massie immediately inform the legislature of the hospital's financial situation.[36]

Stribling's concern for insane persons held in prisons had not diminished. He believed that at least two-thirds of them could have been restored to sanity if they had been treated early, then the heavy expense of supporting them in prisons would have been avoided. Humanity and policy combined to urge the speedy enlargement of Virginia's hospitals to afford relief to those unfortunate people.

While on a trip in 1841, when Stribling found himself close to a prison, he decided to visit it. After witnessing the plight of the insane there, he felt it was his duty to describe their plight to his directors. He wrote "one of the prisoners was a young foreigner of industrious habits and moral character, who had lost his reason within a short period of time. Stribling found him sitting in a remote corner of his cell on a dirty bag partly filled with straw. A strong chain riveted to his ankle bound him to the floor. The prisoner's features were almost concealed by a long beard that had grown unchecked, giving him a somewhat savage and repulsive appearance. His body and limbs were uncovered except for an old, filthy cloth coat on his shoulders that barely concealed his nakedness. Without uttering a syllable, but with a significant gesture, the prisoner directed Stribling's attention to the chain upon his ankle."

Stribling determined that the prisoner was not a lunatic, and after visiting him, he asked the jailer why the prisoner was fettered. The jailer replied that the prisoner had never been dangerous or violent, but tore his clothes and destroyed his furniture. Stribling suggested that if the jailer made a muff for the prisoner's hands, he could wear clothes and walk about his room. But the jailer was an old man who would not make changes, and Stribling could not persuade him to help the prisoner. He left the cell deeply pained by the spectacle.

Then Stribling visited a cell where he found a second man with long hair and a beard. He too was covered with filthy rags. The heavy chain that fastened him to the floor was only long enough to allow him to lie down on his comfortless bed of boards and blankets. This prisoner suffered the horrors of mental disease, aggravated by physical neglect and torture. The effluvia from his filthy cell prevented Stribling from tarrying long with him. Stribling was shocked to learn that the prisoner had been chained to the floor for more than three years. After that visit, Stribling admitted the individual to Western State. However, because of his long confinement, his lower extremities had become entirely paralyzed.

The last cell that Stribling visited was more revolting than either of the other two. It contained five insane females, three whites and two blacks. One of each color was chained in opposite corners of the room, while the remaining three were permitted during the day to exercise or work in an adjoining passage. Stribling believed that every humane and intelligent individual would have felt deep loathing if they had observed the condition of these women because of their number, sex, color and condition. The jailer received nearly $2,000 a year to take care of his eight prisoners while Stribling could have kept thirteen of them comfortably for that amount of money.

After his visit, Stribling wrote in his report to his directors that surely legislators and their constituents had been ignorant of the hapless condition of their unfortunate fellow citizens. He suggested that the press continuously describe the condition of the insane in prisons to everyone in Virginia. Once aware of their suffering and degradation, the public would sympathize with them. Although, Stribling did not observe any positive results from his pleas, he continued to work for the insane in prisons.[37]

Stribling's concern for any insane person's treatment is revealed in an incident that occurred in 1844. The story began in Nelson County, where a prisoner named Hudson received a gunshot wound in his right thigh, into which a hand might have been laid. His left testicle, torn and not supported, dangled in its descended state, many inches from his body. His left thigh, although not lacerated materially, had been the receptacle of many shots which were lodged near an important artery. After examining Hudson on the day of his injury, Doctors Lyons and McCrary placed a large meal poultice upon his wound without first cleansing or dressing it. Afterward, they told the examining magistrates that they left Hudson to die because they believed him irrevocably injured.

However, Hudson did not die, and a third doctor named Jones was called in. He cleansed the man's wound of all foreign substances, removed the poultices, and applied spirits of turpentine to the wounds. Three days later, yet another doctor named Forbes examined Hudson. He stopped the turpentine, ordered light dressing and constant applications of cold water. The turpentine could violate the wound, and extensive sloughing would involve the femoral artery, causing secondary hemorrhaging. Forbes also feared that the shots that passed near the artery of Hudson's left thigh touched its outer coat. He would have removed the injured testicle when he first visited Hudson, but the inflammation was too severe for him to do so. Forbes planned to remove it later.

Because Doctors Lyon and McCrary believed Hudson would die, and Dr. Jones and Forbes believed he would live, Dr. Forbes became more involved in the case. When officials decided to move Hudson to Staunton, he entreated them in vain to allow him to remain in Nelson County. Therefore, a young sheriff placed Hudson in a vehicle on his back with his hands and feet extended and bound with cord. In the most unpropitious weather, the sheriff drove forty miles over an extremely rough road to Staunton, without allowing Hudson any relief.[38]

When the sheriff and his prisoner arrived at Western State, Dr. Stribling and his directors were horrified that a person in such serious condition, and in excruciating pain, had been brought such a distance. Although the hospital did not have a vacancy, the directors instructed Stribling to find a place for him. The directors immediately wrote a harsh resolution censuring those in Nelson County who had been involved in the incident, and gave a copy of it to the sheriff to take back to them.

On August 20, William Massie, one of the magistrates involved in the incident, wrote Stribling that Nelson County officials were unhappy that Western State's censure implied that they were 'inhuman monsters.' Stribling replied that he could not speak for the directors, but he could relate the circumstances under which their resolution had been enacted. He did not believe it stigmatized anyone as an inhuman monster, or charged anyone with deep depravity. On the contrary, while the directors denounced the incident as an outrage upon humanity, they had not asserted responsibility or motives for the act to any particular person.

Stribling wrote that the directors created the censure resolution because during the move, Hudson had suffered excruciating pain, and his wounds had been uncovered and exposed to ants and flies. If he had been soothed at all, it was only by the contents from his bladder and bowels in which he was compelled to lie. The poor creature, emaciated and enfeebled by his sufferings, and almost exhausted from fatigue and exposure, gave vent to his agony by screams that were heard resoundingly and all who approached him found him loathsome and pitiful. As humane men, the directors had to inquire why such a seriously injured person had been brought such a long distance. Also, the directors questioned why the officials had not, as the law required, ensured that Western State had room for Hudson before they sent him there.

Stribling considered the course pursued by those in Nelson County to not have been a judicious one. Nevertheless, he had not judged the sheriff harshly since he seemed to be a young man of kind feelings. While his treatment of his prisoner appeared cruel, the sheriff's actions resulted from his inexperience, or because he held mistaken notions, also held by many men older than he, as to how to treat the insane. Stribling continued that Hudson was rapidly improving, his mind was calmer but still at times excited by delusions. Although Hudson was watched with vigilance, Stribling still feared that he might escape.[39]

Stribling wrote a second letter to William Massie on September 18, 1844, informing him that indeed, Hudson had escaped. He had given him more freedom after Hudson became more rational, because he had believed Hudson's promise that he would not leave the asylum without a legal discharge. Stribling instantly dispatched two attendants to capture him. They had pursued Hudson to his father-in-law's house, where they saw him. However, when Hudson saw the attendants, he escaped into the mountains. Since Hudson's father-in-law considered him well enough to remain at home, he was unwilling to help return him to the hospital.

Since Stribling believed that Hudson was dangerous, he suggested to Massie that he and other officials in Nelson County capture him and return him to Western State. If Nelson County did not have an officer available to return Hudson there, Stribling would send someone for him. [40]

The story revealed Stribling's basic humanitarianism and powers of persuasion. The Hudson incident could have spun out of control on more than one occasion, yet Stribling calmed all of the participants involved and kept them involved in the process.

Obviously Stribling and his directors were pleased in May of 1850 when Governor Thomas W. Gilmer visited both Eastern State and Western State hospitals in May of 1850 and found them in good order and well managed. He further commented that the hospital's physicians and directors were owed a debt of gratitude for the attention they gave to their patients and the improved treatment they had introduced. Gilmer later reported to the House of Delegates that he regretted that so many of the insane were still in jails to the state's great expense and the patients' detriment.[41]

CHAPTER 5

Contention Between Western State and Eastern State

Since Eastern and Western State were both created and supported by the Virginia legislature, any actions of one affected the other. So, in order to understand the contention between them in the early 1840s, it is helpful to understand the history of Eastern State. It was created in 1770 when the House of Burgesses passed *An Act to Provide for the Support and Maintenance of Idiots, Lunatics and Other Persons of Unsound Minds*. Its preamble closely followed Governor Fauquier's first message to them that stated: "Whereas several persons of insane and disordered minds have been frequently found wandering in different parts of this colony, and no certain provision having been yet made either towards effecting a cure of those whose cases are not become quite desperate, nor for restraining others who may be dangerous to society . . . ."[1]

Eastern State was built in Williamsburg, Virginia and accepted its first patients in the fall of 1773. It was the first hospital built exclusively for the care of the insane in the

British North American colonies. Its directors appointed Dr. John de Sequeyra as visiting physician and James Galt as keeper. Sequeyra was assisted by Doctors John Minson Galt and Philip Barraud until his death in 1795.[2] Eastern State became a family affair when Galt was appointed visiting physician in 1795. He served in this position until his death in 1808 when he was replaced by his son, Dr. Alexander Galt who served the hospital for nearly forty years [3].

From the time Eastern State opened, it accepted patients regardless of their class, color, or length of illness, and admission was based on the date of application. Physicians there maintained their extensive practices and seldom influenced policies affecting the hospital. Although the Court of Directors hired a keeper to administer activities at the hospital, they involved themselves in its day-to-day practices.

By 1834, the Virginia legislature had become concerned about the care patients were receiving at Eastern State. Therefore, they appointed a committee to visit the hospital to investigate both its condition and management. Their efforts were later described in the legislators' 1835 report. The committee commended Eastern State's directors and officers for the cleanliness of the patients and good condition of the hospital. There were no offensive smells, and conditions were generally good.

Then the committee made several suggestions that are summarized below. The officers should separate excited patients from convalescents. Candidates for the poorhouses should be moved to them because the hospital's original charge had been to admit only dangerous and curable persons. Galt and his directors should allow patients to eat at tables, hire more attendants to care for those patients locked in unheated, individual cells, and move seventeen patients housed in a damp cellar elsewhere to protect their health. The hospital's officers rebuffed all of those suggestions. When the committee asked the officers whether further accommodation were necessary to promote patient recoveries, the directors answered, "No."

The committee also wrote that Eastern State's low recovery rates proved that its treatments were therapeutically ineffective, especially when similar hospitals in the nation showed a larger number of discharges. The directors and officers of Eastern State proved uncooperative and considered the committee's investigation intrusive. The hospital seemed in essence a well-regulated prison, where prisoners were fed and clothed, but excluded from all employment and amusement.

Eastern State's directors seemed content with their present situation. Their attitude, as displayed in their own annual reports, and noted in the committee's report, showed a continuing ignorance of moral medicine, which by then had gained acceptance among professionals in the field, and had become established in other hospitals for the insane. The committee concluded that Eastern State would be able to attract prospective curable cases only if it made the changes required to practice moral treatment.[4]

On July 1, 1841, John Minson Galt II replaced his ailing father as chief physician and superintendent of Eastern State, a new title that reflected revisions in Virginia's 1841 law. Another change was those heading the two hospitals would have to be physicians and they could not maintain private practices. (Stribling never had a private practice.) The legislature would appoint the head of the institution instead of the Court of Directors who no longer would hold lifetime appointments.[5]

Galt was a graduate of William and Mary College and the University of Pennsylvania. He was a scholar knowledgeable in science and he knew several languages. At first, Galt appeared more interested in studying, researching, and writing than in practicing medicine. Over time, he wrote several books, and articles that would be published in the *American Journal of Insanity*. Galt was able to pursue those activities because he allowed his keeper to administer the hospital. Nevertheless, Galt dedicated himself to his patients who adored him.

Eastern State's directors had always controlled the daily activities of the hospital and had no intention to give Galt the authority to do so, regardless of what his new job description said. Galt seldom influenced his directors because he lacked the self-confidence to assert himself. He even distanced himself from incidents occurring at his hospital that he could have influenced. It must be remembered that Galt was only twenty-two years old when he assumed his duties with only a small amount of practical experience.

Galt was also slow to take advantage of other opportunities available to him to improve his hospital. For example, for a time, he did not seek advice from other superintendents who would have been more than willing to help him. Nor did he cooperate with the Prison Discipline Society of Boston, a group that evaluated insane asylums. The society reported that Western State had participated and received an excellent review. Eastern State, however, sent them no information and did not publish annual reports that manifested the improvement and usefulness of such hospitals.[6]

However, in 1843, after two years on the job, Galt published his first annual report and also visited nine northern hospitals for the insane, where he found their methods effective. As soon as he returned to Eastern State, Galt began to implement most of their practices. Doing so greatly improved his hospital, especially its patient care.[7] When a committee of the Virginia senate visited Eastern State in 1845, they praised his progress. They had found his hospital in an agreeable and unexpected condition. It was now a worthy charity of which Virginia could be proud. Galt's changes had transformed the condition of both the inmates and the buildings, which were imposing and beautiful. The committee noted:

> Patients' rooms were well lit, heated, and ventilated. Each of the twelve-foot-square cells had an iron bedstead with a neat, clean bed and bedding. In many places, a piece of rag carpeting made by the patient lay by the bedside. The entire establishment was neat, clean and free from odor. There were no instruments of coercion or punishment, nor were any patients chained. The staff was respectable, intelligent, and kindhearted. The patients had a small library, convenient shops where they could work, sufficient wholesome food, warm clothes, and comfortable lodgings. Patients attended religious worship on Sundays. [8]

When patients were ill, Galt attended them both day and night. He instituted occupational therapy, exercise, and amusements for his patients and did not allow anyone to punish them. Instead, Galt adopted the principle that love and devotion most helped a patient.

Nevertheless, Dorothea Dix, a reformer who devoted her life to the care of the insane, found problems at Eastern State when she visited in 1848. She wrote Galt that it seemed to her that the steward, not Galt, was acting as superintendent of the hospital. Even if the steward was an excellent person, whom she apparently had no reason to doubt, the situation was untenable. She noted that neither Galt nor the matron lived at the hospital. Dix complained that the hospital did not have enough competent, educated attendants and nurses with proper mental qualifications. The reformer warned that neither Galt's diligence, nor the pleasant location of his institution, could make up for these institutional defects.[9] Information on Dix can be found in Chapter 6.

Now, with some background on Galt and Eastern State, it will be easier to understand the admission policy controversy between the two hospitals. Stribling had seized an opportunity in 1840 to rewrite the law concerning the treatment of the insane. At first, Galt had not objected to Stribling's revisions. Soon, however, he and others began to questions some of his revisions. Now, both hospitals could accept more curable patients. A controversial change allowed the directors to examine patients who had been in their hospitals for more than a year. Now they could send patients that they deemed incurable back to their hometowns for placement there. Or to an institution that would care for them as it cared for those that had been defined as "idiots."[10]

The 1841 revised law also removed the Blue Ridge Mountains as the boundary line that defined the patient pool for each hospital. Now, an applicant first had to apply to the hospital nearer to where he lived. If that hospital did not have a vacancy, only then could he apply to the other hospital that had to admit him if it had a vacancy.[11]

Stribling"s directors soon became concerned with some

of the changes in the revised law. While at first they had first supported Stribling's changes, after a time, they began to have second thoughts about the section that dealt with the admission of curable and incurable patients and the ability to send them elsewhere. In a letter to the Virginia legislature, they admitted that they had found themselves in embarrassing circumstances when they abandoned the previous admission policy. In giving preference to patients who could be cured, they had been unable to accommodate other applicants. Consequently, they had opened themselves to the charges of being unfair and biased in their administration of a public charity.

Still the directors defended their actions. They asserted that if Western State continued to admit patients in the order of their applications, with no preference given to those who were curable, the hospital would soon be filled with incurable patients. The result would be that the "recent" insane, the group with the greatest potential to be cured would be left in their hopeless state. While their actions could cause many insane persons to languish in prisons; overall, the new policy served the public good.[12]

The confrontation became more volatile after members of the legislature asked Eastern State why Western State was curing more patients than they were. To defend themselves, Galt and his directors complained that the 1841 law had hurt rather than helped them. Problems, they said, increased after the Blue Ridge Mountains was no longer the dividing line for admission, and consequently, they wanted to reinstate it. To prove their point, Eastern State reported that a year earlier, Western State had rejected 120 applicants while Eastern State now had only ninety-seven patients with capacity to care for 120.

After receiving a letter from Galt on the issue in November of 1844, Stribling wrote him that if Western State's directors petitioned for any modification of the penal law that affected either institution, he would notify Galt of their action and seek his views on the subject. Stribling asked Galt to do the same. The two of them could deal with each other frankly in a spirit of compromise, and adjust and reconcile their differences more satisfactorily and profitably than could the legislature.[13]

Galt did not respond to Stribling's letter, and Stribling learned months later that Galt and his directors had recently petitioned the legislature to once again make the Blue Ridge Mountains a dividing line between the two hospitals, as it had formerly been.

On December 12, 1844, R. Givens Fulton, a supporter of Western State and member of the Committee for the Insane formed by the House of Delegates, sent Stribling a copy of Eastern State's petition. Stribling immediately wrote Galt that since Galt had rejected his suggestions concerning admissions, Stribling felt compelled to defend Western State's interest to the legislative committee on asylums.[14]

Then Fulton suggested that admission restrictions be removed from both hospitals, but Galt's supporters quickly opposed it. Eastern State continued to complain that because Western State was filled with the recently ill who could be cured, older chronic patients then applied to Eastern State, and he had to admit them. As a consequence, Galt believed that a great injustice was done to Eastern State because it was left with the incurable patients.[15]

Although Stribling wrote Fulton that he would not disparage Galt, he proceeded to do just that. He stated that

Galt's sustaining report contained important errors, the records of the two institutions did not support some of his statements, and many of Galt's impressions and arguments were unsound. Stribling further asserted that he was disinclined to become a party in a controversy that would inevitably damage both institutions. He believed that the law should remain unchanged because it allowed the citizens of the Commonwealth, who had a vested interest in both institutions, a choice.

Stribling also wrote that Western State had never received blacks because no provision had been made for them. Furthermore, he felt strongly that admitting blacks would harm his patients and his institution. Instead, Stribling argued that a separate building or institution was needed for insane blacks. It should be located in Williamsburg because Eastern State already had black patients, so Stribling took it for granted that they had accommodations for them. Stribling and his directors assured the legislative committee that they would be glad to help relieve the afflictions of the black insane "because none needed their sympathy more."[16]

On January 6, 1845, Stribling wrote to the members of the committee of the insane concerning the geographical division between the two hospitals. He did not believe that the law should be changed. Since both hospitals were dependent on support from the same legislature, any division would operate negatively upon one or the other. Also, Western State was not certain that a majority of the legislature would look out for their interests.

As usual, Stribling referred to the history of the establishment of Eastern State. He asserted that Royal Governor Francis Fauquier, the earliest advocate for Eastern

State's creation, had envisioned able physicians restoring an insane person's lost reason. An early court of directors at Eastern State actually had attempted to exclude untreatable patients from the hospital because the legislature had not intended to alleviate parishes of the expenses of their poor.

Stribling cautioned the legislature not to judge either institution solely by the number of patients it cured. The hospital that annually discharged more curable patients was not necessarily better conducted or more entitled to the confidence of the committee than the one that discharged fewer patients. Circumstances, rather than the management and operation of the institution, determined the effectiveness of the cure.

Instead, the reputation of a hospital for the insane should be based on improvements of their incurable patients. Often, curing a recently insane person only required a change of scenery, association, or his removal to a different climate. However, it took time and the exercise of considerable skill to operate on the mind of a patient who was violent and destructive in order to mitigate the malady, change its character, and render the afflicted patient a quiet, contented and comfortable being. Thus, the institution that did the most for incurables was entitled to the highest degree of credit and confidence.[17]

Galt and his directors were unable to convince the legislature to change the law, although they continued their efforts for some time. Ultimately, their persistence hurt their cause because some legislators believed that Eastern State wanted laws changed in their favor because they could not compete with Western State in patient care. That impression may have been widespread since Western State obtained more paying patients than Eastern State. Indeed, an 1857 report from Western State showed that it received $17,000 to $18,000 in revenue from paying patients while Eastern State only received $2,500.[18]

Many at Eastern State believed that Western State won the admissions battle because Stribling and Western State had more legislative support than they did. In contrast to Galt, Stribling educated the governor and won the favor of the state legislators by sending them Western State's annual reports, establishing personal relationships, and welcoming them to visit their hospital. Therefore, some bitterness continued between the two hospitals.

Later, Eastern State created a "refusal form," and declared that it was the only verification that it would accept from Western State that it did not have a vacancy. Stribling refused to sign it and argued that the directors of Eastern State were remiss in initiating it because the law did not refer to a form. Thus a letter from Stribling should suffice. Such bickering over procedures between the two hospitals confused families and friends of the insane, as well as the jailers transporting them.[19] Ultimately, Eastern State's cause was damaged before the legislature.

It was not surprising that Stribling and Galt reacted differently to the admissions controversy. While the two men were similar in some respects, they were quite different in others. Both came from well-known and affluent families, Stribling had ten siblings while Galt had one brother and two sisters. Both were young when they assumed their responsibilities, Stribling, twenty-six and Galt, twenty-two. Both obtained medical degrees from the University of Pennsylvania, cared deeply for their patients, and were among the thirteen founders of the superintendents' association. Stribling devoted all of his intellect and energies to Western State and was involved in every detail that affected it. Galt cared for his patients, but preferred scholarly pursuits, leaving the administration of his hospital to his keeper.

At first, Galt protested when Stribling persuaded his directors to admit paying patients. Soon, however, he changed his mind and asked Stribling for his advice on how to initiate a similar policy at Eastern State. In 1843, Eastern State took actions to attract paying patients. For example, Galt placed an ad in a Florida newspaper and also issued circulars soliciting patients that included endorsements from President John Tyler, the Episcopal bishop of Virginia, and the president of the College of William and Mary. He also tried, somewhat unsuccessfully, to stop some members of his staff from competing with the hospital by accepting paying patients in their homes for private treatment.[20]

IMAGE 2

Stribling Springs. Built in 1817 by Erasmus Stribling. From *Album of Virginia*, Author Edward Beyer,
Illustrated by Edward Beyer.
(Courtesy, University of Virginia Library.)

ALICE DAVIS WOOD

IMAGE 3

University of Virginia, 1827.
Engraving by Tanner.
(Courtesy, University of Virginia Library.)

IMAGES 4A, 4B, 4C

Graduation note cards issued by professors of the
University of Pennsylvania to Stribling.
(Courtesy, University of Virginia Library.)

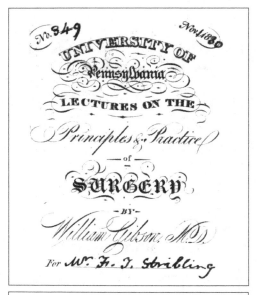

IMAGES 5A, 5B, 5C

Graduation note cards issued by professors of the
University of Pennsylvania to Stribling.
(Courtesy, University of Virginia Library.)

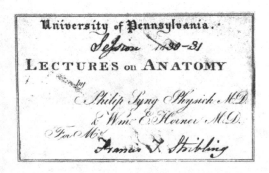

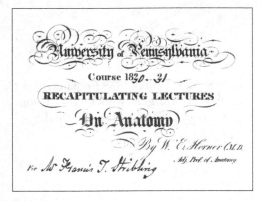

IMAGES 6A, 6B, 6C

Graduation note cards issued by professors of the
University of Pennsylvania to Stribling.
(Courtesy, University of Virginia Library.)

IMAGE 7

Western State Hospital, 1838.Prepared by A.C.
Smith from an original work by R.C. Long.
(Courtesy, Western State Hospital.)

IMAGE 8

Western State Hospital, Date Unknown.
(Courtesy, Western State Hospital.)

To the friends of the Insane.

THE Directors of the Virginia Lunatic Asylum, at Williamsburg, would inform the public of the Southern States that, by a recent law of the Legislature, they are empowered to receive insane patients, paying board, from other States. This is the oldest Institution of the kind in the Union, having been founded by the Colonial Government in 1769; and is, from its location, best adapted for Southerners, being removed from the piercing cold of the North, and from the enervating heat of the South. Its curative capacity is of the highest order: nine out of ten cases recover, if received within the first six months of the disease. It is easy of access, as steamers daily stop at a wharf not far from the Asylum. The modern treatment, upon the non-restraint system, is in successful operation. The apartments admit of classification of patients according to their state of mind, and also a complete division of the classes of society. The fare is excellent, and the board $4 per week. We have neat bed-rooms, a parlor tastefully furnished with curtains, carpet, sofa, centre-table, ottomans, mirrors, books and a piano: airy verandahs for summer retreats; an extensive enclosure for evening rambles; a carriage for morning and evening rides; a reading room furnished with books and newspapers; and moreover various means of amusement.— A Chaplain resides in the building and preaches to the patients every Sabbath. Letters of inquiry should be directed to Dr. JOHN M. GALT, Physician and Superintendent of the Eastern Asylum, Williamsburg, Virginia.

March 14, 1846.

IMAGE 9

Newspaper Advertisement.
Used by Eastern State in the 1840s to attract paying
patients. It appeared in a Florida newspaper.
(Courtesy, Eastern State Hospital.)

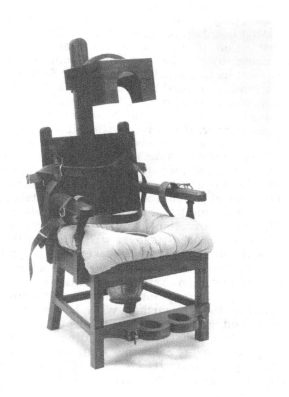

IMAGE 10

Restraining Chair.
Not favored during the moral medicine era.
(Courtesy, Colonial Williamsburg Foundation)

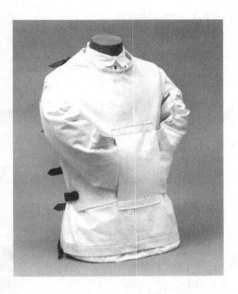

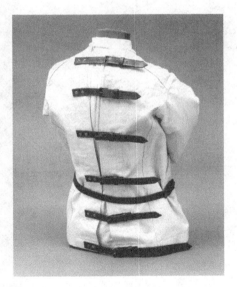

IMAGES 11, 12

Straightjacket, front and back views.
Not favored during the moral medicine era.
(Courtesy, Colonial Williamsburg Foundation)

IMAGE 13

Utica Crib.
This restraining device appeared in the late 1800s
and reflected the demise of moral medicine.
(Courtesy, Western State Hospital.)

IMAGES 14A and 14B

Wristband and Mittens.
Not favored by most physician during the
moral medicine era.
(Courtesy, Colonial Williamsburg Foundation.)

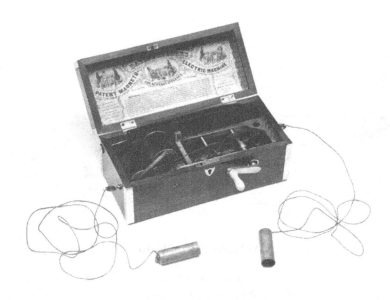

IMAGE 15

Davis and Kidder Electric Machine.
As a treatment, used to electrify patients.
(Courtesy, Western State Hospital.)

IMAGE 16

Spinning Wheel used by female patients at Western State.
(Courtesy, Western State Hospital.)

IMAGE 17

Dress made by female patients at Western State.
Details include pulled thread accent work and crocheting.
(Courtesy, Western State Hospital.)

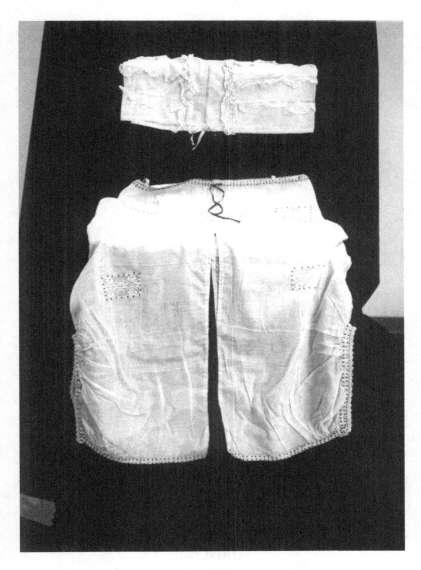

IMAGE 18

Undergarment made by female patients at Western State.

Details as described in image above.

(Courtesy, Western State Hospital.)

IMAGE 19

Lancets.
Used to bleed insane patients and others who were ill.
(Courtesy, Colonial Williamsburg Foundation.)

IMAGE 20

Glyster
During the 1800s, doctors often evacuated their
patients bowels with glysters and syringes.
(Courtesy, Colonial Williamsburg Foundation.)

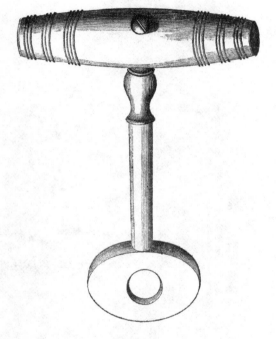

IMAGE 21

Feeding Device
Used to force patients to eat. Developed by
John Haslam of Bethlehem Hospital in the 1800s.
(Courtesy, Colonial Williamsburg Foundation.)

IMAGE 22

Three-wheel chair.
Front view.
(Courtesy, Western State Hospital.)

IMAGE 23

Three-wheel chair.
(Side view.)
Courtesy, Western State Hospital.)

IMAGE 24

Trunk.
(Courtesy, Western State Hospital.)

IMAGE 25

Patients' Chair with side tray.
(Courtesy, Western State Hospital.)

IMAGE 26

Violins, battledores (racquets), shuttlecocks,
dominoes and playing cards. Items used by
patients in the 1800s.
(Courtesy of Colonial Williamsburg.)

IMAGE 27

Accordion.
(Courtesy, Western State Hospital.)

IMAGE 28

Ediphone.
(Courtesy, Western State Hospital.)

IMAGE 29

Chapel at Western State built in early 1850s.
(Courtesy, Western State Hospital.)

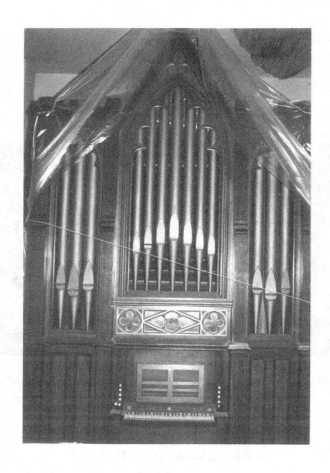

IMAGE 30

Organ given to Western State Hospital by
W. W. Cocoran in the early 1850s.
(Courtesy, Western State Hospital.)

IMAGE 31

View of the organ showing damage by the
environment, falling ceiling, and birds.
(Courtesy, Western State Hospital.)

IMAGE 32

Portrait of Dr. John Minson Galt II.
Painted by Francis Miller White.
(Courtesy, Eastern State Hospital.)

IMAGE 33

View of Eastern State Hospital, 1850s.
(Courtesy, Colonial Williamsburg Foundation.)

ENGRAVED BY R. G. TIETZE.

DOROTHEA L. DIX.

IMAGE 34

Dorothea Dix from engraving by R.G. Tietze.
(Courtesy, University of Virginia Library.)

CHAPTER 6

Dorothea Dix and Dr. Francis T. Stribling–

An Intense Friendship

D orothea Lynde Dix was a towering figure in the nineteenth-century reform movement. Known as a crusader for the pauper insane, she became one of the most politically active and well-traveled women of her time. Dix was directly responsible for founding or enlarging thirty-two mental hospitals in fifteen states, Canada, Britain, Europe, and Japan.[1] She also was involved in the creation of the Government Hospital for the Insane in Washington D. C., [2] fifteen schools for the feeble-minded, a school for the blind, and numerous training schools for nurses.[3] Her traumatic New England beginnings shaped the course her life would take.

Dix was born in Hampden, Maine, on April 4, 1802, into an itinerant Methodist minister's family. Her father, who was often away on church matters, was an abusive alcoholic and her mother was unstable. For those reasons Dix assumed the responsibility for her two younger brothers as the family moved throughout New England and gradually disintegrated. When she was twelve years old it became clear that neither parent could care for their children, and her wealthy grandmother intervened. She brought the children to her home in Boston and sent their parents to stay with relatives.

Dix's grandmother tried without success to prepare her granddaughter for Boston society, because Dix was not interested. With the help of her cousin, Edward Bangs, Dix opened a school for girls in Worcester. Later she opened a boarding school for them in Boston and also created a class for poor girls at the Dix mansion.

Dix first saw incarcerated insane persons in 1841 when she was thirty-nine years old after she volunteered to teach a Sunday School class to female inmates of the East Cambridge jail. The images she saw changed her life forever: prostitutes, drunks, criminals, insane persons, and men were all housed together in unheated, unfurnished, and foul-smelling quarters. Dix rejected the commonly held notions that the insane did not feel heat or cold or that their abysmal living conditions were good enough for them. Although Dix thought some of the insane could not be cured, she knew intuitively that better living conditions would benefit them.

Determined to help those afflicted people, Dix surveyed the living conditions of the insane both inside and outside of prisons in Boston, and then those living in the rest of Massachusetts. Afterwards, she placed the data she had gathered into a petition and presented it to the Massachusetts legislature. Finally, Dix argued that Worcester State Hospital be expanded to admit them, after a heated debate, the legislature funded her project. Her intelligence, determination, and passion to do whatever was necessary to help the insane had impressed the legislature.

It helped her cause that Dix was a good friend with the governor and his secretary. Dix continued her crusade by then turning her attention to the plight of the insane in other states. Over time, her travels would take her to every state east of the Mississippi River. In all of those places, she employed the same strategy: survey prisons and almshouses, prepare a petition, present it to the legislatures, and go to court when necessary.[4] Although Dix did not storm legislative halls, she worked tirelessly to bring the cause of the insane to both lawmakers and the public. She even invited anyone who was interested to visit her in her boardinghouse for further discussions.

> Among them were philanthropists, political leaders, and public officials who acknowledged her supremacy in such affairs. Some evenings, she had, at the same time, 20 gentlemen for three hours of steady conversation. With those who were recalcitrant, Dix explained, expostulated, and entreated on behalf of the helpless insane, as though her life depended on the issue.[5]

Therefore, Dix educated her audience about her cause and persuasively argued her point of view at a time when women were not supposed to have a public life. Yet, no one questioned her moral character because she was a model of propriety, by nature quiet, soft-spoken, dignified and modest. At the same time, Dix was confident, and "while she did not excite passions or blame others for the misery she found, she was serious and persistent." Dix always wore a simple black or gray dress with only a touch of white at the neck. Her head was finely set and shaped with an abundance of brown wavy hair. One of her students once said that next to her mother, Dix was the most beautiful woman she had ever known.[6]

The most ambitious project Dix ever engaged in, and one that continued for several years, was to persuade Congress to become involved in the care and treatment of the insane poor. To that end, she petitioned the United States Congress in 1854 to sell twelve million acres of public land and set aside the proceeds for the care of the insane across the nation. After working on the project for eight years, Congress passed the bill. However, President Franklin Pierce, a states-rightist, vetoed it.[7] Because of her work, Dix was highly regarded by the superintendents, who more than most, understood the value of her work. She was also a close friend with some of them so it was understandable that they supported her efforts. Yet, it gave Dix little comfort that the superintendents noted in their annual report that they appreciated her motives, labors and untiring perseverance, and regretted that her bill had not been passed.[8] In advocating her causes to the federal government, Dix was a woman ahead of her time.

Throughout her life Dix had health problems. Years earlier, when she had suffered a severe bout of illness, she traveled to Europe to recuperate. Now, completely devastated by the bill's defeat and exhausted by years of working on it, she became too ill to work. Once again she returned to England where friends there helped her recover. After her health improved, Dix remained in Europe for two years and took her crusade for the insane to Scotland and the Channel Islands. In Rome, she interceded with Pope Pius IX on their behalf. Dix eventually visited Greece, Turkey, Austria-Hungary, Germany, Russia, and the Scandinavian countries, working tirelessly to change the ways Europeans dealt with their insane persons.[9]

Dorothea Dix and Stribling had in common their desire to relieve the suffering of the insane, and that became the foundation of their friendship. Their correspondence began in 1849 and ended in 1860. Dix wrote Stribling twenty letters and he wrote her seven. In those letters, they shared their unfettered thoughts on many subjects. Both of them also supported an institution now called the Virginia School for the Deaf and the Blind. Efforts to establish the school had begun in 1826 in Richmond. By 1833, local citizens lobbied to have it placed in Staunton, and that location also was advocated by Stribling and Dr. Lewis Chamberlayne of Richmond. The school finally became a reality in 1838.

Their friendship deepened in the 1850s when Stribling helped Dix place several afflicted young women in the school. Often, Dix brought them to Staunton, and afterwards, Stribling wrote her detailed letters on their progress. The two of them became even closer while Dix traveled to the southern states and lobbied state legislators there to build new hospitals for the insane. Perhaps because Stribling understood southern politics, was an excellent doctor, and had created the type of hospital that Dix endorsed, she frequently turned to him for advice on a variety of subjects: hospital sites and construction, proposed superintendents, patient treatment, and others. Dix frequently asked Stribling to send information to the recently hired, often young, and inexperienced superintendents of the newly created hospitals.

Now and then Dix purchased items for Stribling during her travels. In a letter dated January 11, 1859, he described a stereoscope that he had recently received from her. "The instrument seems a good one and the views on the slides are handsome. With proper regulation, the officers can make the stereoscope interesting and useful to the patients, especially those who can not attend exhibitions with the magic lanterns."[10] Dix also included in the package articles from the *American Sunday School Union* and prints from *Earle of Philadelphia*. Stribling sent Dix a check for the money that the hospital owed her for the purchases.

Despite her reputation as a social reformer, Dix never became associated with abolition or suffrage movements. Although she must have believed in those causes, she had the discipline and foresight to remain entirely focused on her own work. She understood that her image could be severely damaged were she to take a public stand on slavery. Dix could not afford to alienate the very legislators whose help she needed, especially those in the South.

It is not known how often Dix and Stribling discussed what must have been their opposing views on slavery. They may have wanted to avoid an emotional issue that had the potential to damage their friendship. Their letters that survive only include one that mentions blacks, when Stribling, obviously responding to a question from Dix, described Western State's admission policy concerning them. He wrote that he had never recommended admitting blacks into his institution. Instead, he urged the legislature to provide separate facilities for them. However, after Galt offered to provide for them at Eastern State, without additional expenditures for buildings, the legislature, always unwilling to appropriate money if they could avoid it, adopted his plan.[11]

Dix immediately took action when she strongly disagreed with an issue. For example, she was extremely displeased to learn that the superintendents planned to consider at their next meeting, a policy to allow male attendants to work on female patients' wards. She immediately wrote Stribling and requested him to use his influence to defeat that proposal, because she was too busy to attend their meeting personally to protest. Dix continued that she could not condone an action that transgressed propriety. She concluded that it was fortunate that their medical colleagues already had expressed their indignation that Doctors Woodward and Charles presently permitted this practice. Other superintendents would support efforts by Stribling to end the practice before it became standard. She urged Stribling to address the matter as quickly as possible.[12]

Stribling apparently agreed with Dix that the new policy should be rejected and he raised the issue at the 1852 meeting of the superintendents' association. He stated that he had experience with more than 500 insane females, and never once had called in a male attendant to help control a female patient. Doing so was unnecessary and unwise. He advised that "Such a practice would outrage public opinion and violate the modesty that was a virtue most important to the female character. It would tend to aggravate the distress and anxiety of the already heartbroken parents, husbands, and brothers on behalf of a cherished daughter, wife or sister."

Stribling was unaware of a similar policy in other hospitals for the insane. Since he could not imagine any reason for such policy, he contented himself with endorsing the views so forcibly and admirably expressed a day or two earlier by their associate, Dr. Ray.[13]

Stribling's correspondence with Dix seemed to have ended in 1860, perhaps the victim of the deepening sectional crisis. When the rising tensions between the North and South erupted into Civil War, she put her energies into being the

Superintendent of Union Army Nurses, a capacity in which she served until the war's end. She also wrote young Frank Stribling while he was a prisoner of war and offered to help him.

Dorothea Dix died on July 17, 1887 at the New Jersey State Hospital in Trenton.

CHAPTER 7

Charges of Patient Abuse at Western State

On October 15, 1852, Stribling accidentally saw a pamphlet written by Captain V.M. Randolph of the United States Navy entitled, *A Candid Inquiry Into Some of the Abuses and Cruelties Now Existing and Practiced in the Staunton, Virginia Insane Asylum, Together with A Few Humble Suggestions For Their Correction*. Within the pamphlet, that he had sent to the Virginia Legislature, Randolph stated that abuses were taking place at Western State. Furthermore, by describing them, it was more likely that the legislators would more thoroughly examine its two hospitals for the insane. Randolph described the treatment that his deranged son had received while a patient at Western State, based on his conversations with patients there.[1]

As soon as they read the pamphlet, Stribling and his directors understood that the charges could possibly have a detrimental effect on their reputations and that of their hospital. Especially if the charges were believed either by the legislature, relatives of patients, or the general public.[2] Abridgements of the documentation describing the event follow.

Some time after Randolph's twenty-five-year-old son, who lived in Alabama, became deranged, his younger brother, a physician, took him to Baltimore and had him admitted to the Mount Hope Asylum. Soon Randolph traveled to Baltimore to visit him and was alarmed to find his son in an enfeebled and emaciated condition. Doctors there informed Randolph that his son might be attempting to commit suicide by refusing to eat. But Randolph suspected other reasons for his son's condition, especially after he discovered that his son had been choked by a hospital attendant, described by patients who had witnessed the event as a rough, brutal Irishman.[3]

Randolph moved his son to Western State in May of 1852 after it had been recommended to him as an institution with an excellent cure rate. Furthermore, he wanted his son in a Protestant institution. Thus began the confrontation between Randolph and Stribling. As soon as his son was settled, Randolph, who suffered from poor health, decided to take a short vacation. After a time, with no word from Stribling as to his son's condition, Randolph returned to Staunton. As soon as he arrived, he visited Stribling who told him that the sobering fact was that his son was more emaciated and deranged than he had been when he had been admitted.

Randolph immediately visited his son and found him housed in a different room, his arms strapped to a chair, and in a state of heightened agitation.[4] Bruises on his body had apparently been caused when he had thrown himself violently onto the floor and against the walls of his room. When his son saw his father, he burst into a passion of tears, demanding to know why he had been abandoned to die in a madhouse.[5]

Randolph immediately attempted to see Stribling but he was unavailable. Subsequently, he wrote him a letter complaining about his son's treatment. Then Randolph asked Stribling if he would could sleep at night should one of his own children be so ill-treated.[6] Furthermore, Randolph requested that Stribling move his son to his former room, and provide an American attendant to care for him. Also, he informed Stribling that as soon as his son's health permitted, he planned to move him back to Alabama, where his slaves could care for him.[7] Near the end of his letter, Randolph described to Stribling other incidents of patient abuse based on what he had been told by patients.[8]

Stribling responded to Randolph in a letter on July 20, 1852. Were his own son ill, he wrote, he would have acted as Randolph had. But in addition, he would have supplied him with a faithful nurse, whose sole duty would have been to watch and aid his son. But, had he been unable to procure a nurse, he would have slept quietly, knowing that he had done all he could under the circumstances to care for and comfort his child. Nevertheless, Stribling agreed to move Randolph's son back to his former room. At the same time, he felt compelled to defend his employees, assuring Randolph they had done all that they could for his son. And even though Randolph lacked confidence in them, he and his employees would continue to provide him with good care.[9] Stribling then asked Randolph not to talk to his other patients on subsequent visits.

Stribling's response did not pacify Randolph, and in his reply to Stribling, he asserted that it appeared to him that Stribling was insinuating that his son's mistreatment was Randolph's fault because he had not supplied a servant to guard him against injury.[10] He questioned, if only those who furnished servants had the right to complain when their relatives were neglected. Randolph went on to say that he had paid seventeen dollars a month for his son's care at the hospital and he assumed that care protected him from injury and suffering. Randolph did not believe that he should have to pay ten dollars more for a servant but he would do so in order to protect his son.

Also, Randolph expressed outrage that Stribling's requested that he not talk to other patients and asked "And has it come to this? Were poor creatures shut out from the world to be denied talking to a visitor who might have an interest in them?"[11] Randolph concluded his letter by warning Stribling that were his "inquisitorial restrictions and sentiments" widely known, they would erode his reputation for kindness and "might cause those who were skeptical to avoid moving relatives and friends into hospitals for treatment."[12]

By now, Stribling had become impatient with Randolph and attempted to dismiss him. In a terse response, he disagreed with Randolph's views and informed him that any further correspondence on the matter was useless and a waste of his time.[13] Later, when Stribling and Randolph met, Randolph levied more accusations of abuse. A patient named Leven said that when another patient named Dr. Hall, either by accident or negligence, threw coffee on the walls of his room that had recently been whitewashed, Attendant O'Meara cruelly choked him for more than a minute. Samuel Hashour, another attendant, with the help of a servant boy named Robert, dragged Hall downstairs, undressed him, and showered him for more than a quarter of an hour. Terrified, Hall screamed for mercy. From then on, Hall's mind grew worse, and he became so desperate that he attempted to kill himself by jumping out of a window. But he succeeded only in spraining his ankle.[14]

Leven also claimed to have observed the suffering and death of another patient, who remained on the floor of his room for more than two hours before dying in the midst of his own filth. Leven and other patients wanted to help him but were unable to do so. In addition, another a patient named McCowan said that when he told O'Meara that he was too ill to eat, the attendant threatened to use a stomach tube to force the food down his throat. Other patients described attendants practicing immoralities that exceeded all bounds, neglecting patients while engaging "in beastly debauchery with the Negro wenches of the establishment." With tears in his eyes, another patient told Randolph that "he dreaded that he might become deranged and confined under the mercy of unfeeling attendants."[15]

In response, Stribling cautioned Randolph that his evidence came from delusional madmen and he also questioned why had patients not described those abuses to him, so that he might investigate them.

In defense of his sources, Randolph accused Stribling of knowing that many of his patients were not, in any sense of the word, mad. He further claimed that patients had told him of abuses only to help him protect his son, and that any humane and truth-loving person would believe them. The sad fact was that patients were afraid to tell Stribling anything because his confidence in his attendants and doctors was so unshakable that he would not have believed them. The pity was that patients believed that "they would have offended Stribling and also incurred the ill will of the attendants who had great power to vex and persecute them." Then Randolph

accused Stribling of making statements that he knew were
not true because "he might want to controvert them on a
future occasion." Irate by now, Randolph finally "proclaimed
that his son had been at the mercy of a heartless and
disingenuous person, and he felt no respect for Stribling, who
had deceived him."[16]

As part of his efforts to discredit Stribling and Western
State, Randolph then wrote two letters to Dorothea Dix in a
futile attempt to obtain her support, wherein he described
even more details of patient abuse at Western State. As an
example, a servant had told Randolph that Attendant Hashour
had bruised his son's mouth with a key that he used to force
him to take his medicine. His son, who had been listening,
exclaimed, "Yes, they drenched me like a horse."[17]
Furthermore, when Randolph complained to Stribling, he was
told that the key was appropriate for the purpose. Stribling
also told the distraught father that he had unlimited confidence
in Hashour, who was one of the most tenderhearted nurses to
be found anywhere.[18] Also, according to Stribling, his
attendants knew that they would be dismissed if they struck
a patient. Then, Randolph continued that "Stribling said
nothing about the practice of mashing patients' heads against
the wall." Among other things, Randolph's son had told him
that he had been subjected to that abuse.[19]

Randolph then wrote that his son had died on August 26,
1852 after being at the hospital for three months. Since then,
Randolph had often thanked God that his son had been in
full possession of his mental faculties for thirty-six hours prior
to his death. During that time, lucid conversations with him
consoled Randolph, except when his son described his
treatment at Western State. Almost the last words he spoke

were to a younger brother then weeping over him. "My brother, I am in my senses now and father ought not have brought me here."[20]

In that same letter, Randolph complained to Dix that Stribling's numerous and strong family connections shielded him from scrutiny. Also, he disbursed large sums of public money and received money from paying patients. And, of course, Stribling belonged to the Episcopal Church, as did his directors and the merchants and others that he patronized. Anyone who said anything against Western State at once incurred the displeasure of all the Episcopalians in Staunton, "as I had seen and felt to my sorrow."[21] Furthermore, Stribling would not allow clergymen to visit his son, and he also had attempted to keep the public in utter ignorance as to what was happening in his hospital.[22] Also, Stribling also did not hire enough servants to keep the hospital clean.[23] Among other things, when Dix had been a guest in Stribling's home on a visit to Staunton while Randolph was there, Stribling never gave him an opportunity to meet her, although he knew that Randolph desired to do so, and his boarding house was close to Stribling's residence.[24]

Soon after the directors learned from Stribling that Randolph had written the pamphlet, they formed a committee from their own members to investigate them. It consisted of James H. Rimer, William A. Abrie, and Thomas Eskridge.[25]

In late December, the committee took depositions from a former patient, two former attendants, a current attendant, the assistant physician, and two local religious leaders. Abridgements from their testimony follow. Patient McCowan stated that Randolph had correctly described the incident with Attendant O'Meara. However, it had been a patient named

Leven who claimed that he had observed patients driven to despair from cruel treatment, and saw some die from want of kindness. But yet, McCowan had seen O'Meara abruptly take a patient by the throat, whose only offense was going outside after it had rained, and shoved him into a building. Further, McCowan had never insisted on being discharged, nor had he ever believed that he was kept in the hospital because he was a paying patient. [26]

Attendants Patrick McNamara, Caleb Crone, and Hashour understood that they did not have authority to shower or restrain patients; however, sometimes they did, and later described the incidents to the officers. Once in the past, after McNamara had struck a patient who annoyed him, Stribling warned him that he would be discharged if a similar incident occurred. McNamara also attested that Stribling had earlier fired two attendants: one who injured an escaped patient and another who was drunk. Hashour was certain that he could not have unmercifully showered Hall for fifteen minutes, without remembering it. All the attendants attested that Stribling visited his patients every day, and that little escaped his attention. They agreed that Stribling had to trust in his staff, because "no man under the sun could manage an institution such as theirs unless he could place confidence in the integrity of the attendants under him."[27]

Dr. William Hamilton, the asylum's assistant physician, testified that if former patient Levin had seen a patient struggling with an attendant, "or in a situation that aroused his sympathy, he might become too excited to accurately observe and correctly report the incident."[28] Finally, two local ministers refuted Randolph's charge that the clergy were not allowed to visit patients.[29]

The committees' report to the director on January 5, 1853 stated that it had used all of its power to determine whether or not the alleged abuses and cruelties had occurred. It was sorry about the misfortunes experienced by Randolph and believed that his "motive was to help those in whose cause he had taken an interest. At the same time, they disagreed with Randolph as to the effect his pamphlet produced." [30]

The committee believed that a person engaged in a candid conversation with a deranged person should consider with caution statements made by him. According to the committee, Randolph had erred when he gave credence to everything the patients said that was disadvantageous to the hospital.[31]

The committee continued that it had given a great deal of credence to Dr. Hamilton who had been in young Kendall's room several times on the day he died, first alone and later with Stribling. Hamilton saw nothing that led him to suspect that Kendall was not receiving proper care. Nevertheless, the committee had been astonished by the charge that attendants at Western State had treated patients cruelly. After all, Hashour was a reliable and worthy young man who would never have harmed a patient. Even more important, over the years, hundreds of patients, some very ill, had been admitted to the hospital and returned home cured. Not one of them had ever made an accusation against the hospital.[32]

Without notifying Stribling, the committee visited both rooms occupied by Randolph. In spite of Randolph's accusations to the contrary, they concluded that the first room occupied by his son was preferable to the one where he had been moved. Nor did it believe there was any difference between the two rooms.

Because Dr. Stribling visited sick patients once each day and the assistant physician visited them twice,[33] patients had ample opportunities to describe abuse to the doctors. Furthermore, had violence occurred, it would have left its mark; had improper confinement been alleged, its truth could have readily been determined; and had restraints had been placed on patients, the means necessary to do so would have been visible.[34] As to restraints, common sense required that Randolph be protected, even if doing so for a time, denied him the use of his arms. Consequently, in Randolph's case, Stribling had no choice but to disregard the usual rules of moral treatment concerning restraints.

The committee did not believe that the testimony of patients should be discarded altogether, because there were many patients whose judgement the officers considered in forming opinions, and in whom they had great confidence. It did not believe, however, that such great abuses and cruelties were likely to exist, or existed and not be discovered. Among all of the employees at the hospital, at least one would not have permitted such abuses and cruelties to continue, and would have been honest and humane enough to expose them to the public.[35]

On the other hand, the committee knew enough about many of the unhappy patients to understand that even the best run institution might be hopelessly destroyed if its character were dependent upon the statements made by many of its inmates. The sad fact was that many patients were brought to the hospital believing that their nearest relatives and best friends were their deadliest enemies. And therefore, some patients bitterly reproached them.[36] As to Randolph's claim that the hospital was unclean, the committee had visited the hospital without notice, and gone through every portion of it without an officer. In all essentials, the charge that the hospital was unclean were unfounded.[37]

Certainly, the committee did not pretend to say that instances of negligence and misconduct did not occur. But it was well known that the hospital had always practiced diligent supervision and punished those responsible when delinquencies had been discovered. Accordingly, the committee concluded that Captain Randolph's pamphlet was unnecessary and his accusations unfounded. It was unfortunate that his accusations had the potential to do a great deal of damage to the hospital. The committee had already heard that the pamphlet had been maliciously circulated to friends and relatives of inmates of the hospital, producing a great deal of discontent among many. Thus, the committee felt it its duty to recommend that the directors call the matter to the attention of the legislature. If it chose to investigate the charges, the committee promised them its full cooperation. In the end, however, no further investigation was conducted.[38]

On January 8, 1853, the court of directors received, read, and unanimously adopted the committee's report and appointed another committee to prepare another report for the Virginia legislature. They were astonished to find such grave charges published in a pamphlet sent throughout the state. Randolph, a man of high standing and reputation, had left their midst to publicize his accusations, without sending those same accusations to the court of directors, the constituted guardians of the institution.

The directors agreed with the committee that it was not proper to take evidence of patients still in the hospital and uncured. "It was not probable that such testimony would reveal the truth, as was shown by Captain Randolph's own imperfections in that line."

If the legislature did not further investigate the charges, the directors and their committee urged that both houses at least investigate the condition and management of the hospital. Anything they found wrong would be corrected. If it was all right, let the people of the state, and especially the friends of the unfortunate patients have the assurance that only the legislature could give. They encouraged more visits to the hospital. Travel between Richmond and Staunton at that time was easy and pleasurable.[39]

Undoubtedly, Stribling and his directors must have been appalled and humiliated by Randolph's charges. If believed, the families and friends of the patients, the Virginia General Assembly and the general public could quickly lose faith in him and in Western State. Therefore, they must have felt it important to quickly refute each and every charge made by Randolph, and they did.

On the other hand, when Stribling did not allow his patients to testify, he broke the fragile trust with them that he had carefully nurtured over the years. After all, he and his directors knew that many of the patients were capable of giving accurate and truthful testimony, especially those who would soon be discharged. Nevertheless, in their panic, Stribling and his directors appeared to be afraid to subject the hospital's officers and attendants to the close scrutiny that a thorough investigation would have required.

There is no doubt that the committee rushed to judgement. The charges of abuse of Randoloph's son occurred in the late spring and early summer of 1852; he died in August;

Randolph published his pamphlet in the fall; depositions were completed by December 27; and the directors had read and approved the committee's report by January 5, 1853.

It seems apparent that Stribling trusted his employees too much. Because he knew that there had been instances of abuse by attendants in the past, deep down, he must have known there was a possibility that it could happen again. At least some of Randolph's charges, therefore, could possibly be true. Also, the Committee well understood that they had rushed the investigation. According to their own statement near the end of the report when it wrote "that its testimony was submitted together with its feeble and hasty review of a portion of it." Thus, for that reason, it appears that the committee had little faith in its own investigation or else it was trying to save itself from future criticism.

So far, evidence has not surfaced that Dix ever answered Randolph's letters. However, her reaction to the investigation was revealed in a letter that Stribling wrote to her on March 8, 1853. He wrote that he was "glad that Dix believed that Western State had disposed of Captain Randolph properly. The old gentleman, however, was affixed with that troublesome (to others) malady. They would not be surprised to find, in print, before long, a response to their pamphlet from him."[40]

CHAPTER 8

The Demise of Moral Medicine in

Virginia and Elsewhere

O vercrowded hospitals would become one of the major reasons for the demise of moral medicine because it gradually destroyed one of its most important tenets: a close relationship between the patient and his caretaker. In 1849, Stribling wrote that he was in dire need of more accommodations. He reminded his directors that while they had provided rooms for more patients, few had been added for officers, employees, and servants. Consequently, urgently needed were additional sleep rooms for assistant physicians; accommodations for servants, chambers for the housekeeper, an office for the steward, and store rooms for dry goods and wholesale purchases. Also, it was necessary to either build new buildings or enlarge existing ones for the kitchen, bakery, pantry, library room, dining room, and chapel.[1]

Because other superintendents in the nation were experiencing similar problems, in May of 1851, their association unanimously resolved that no more than 250 patients could be treated properly in one building, although

200 was the ideal population. Unfortunately, by then Politics would override their efforts to make changes. By 1855, Western State contained 404 patients because Stribling and his directors had been unwilling to reject applicants.

The following correspondence between Stribling and his directors, and between him and the Governor of Virginia, are probably representative of what was happening throughout the nation. He admitted to his directors in 1854 that he had been wrong to suggest and encourage the constant enlargement of his hospital. To atone for that serious error, Stribling promised to use his influence in Virginia and elsewhere, to prevent any hospital for the insane from being constructed for more than 250 patients.

At that time, Western State contained 149 single rooms and eighty-three associate dormitories, each with two to seven beds. Severely ill patients occupied the single rooms until they improved, then Stribling placed them in the dormitories. Still, said Stribling, he exercised great care not to place homicidal, noisy, or filthy patients into an apartment occupied by two, three, or four quiet, genteel, orderly patients, however disordered their intellect.

Stribling, however, remained under pressure to admit more patients even though his hospital did not have room for them. For example, Governor Wise's secretary wrote him on July 1, 1857, that the governor had repeatedly received complaints that Stribling refused applicants and showed partiality in accepting others. The governor wanted to know the present number of patients and vacancies, and how many applicants had been refused admission over the past six months.[2]

In his reply to the governor, Stribling admitted that since it was impossible to accommodate all applicants to the hospital, he accepted the recent insane over the chronic insane and the poor over the rich. He reminded the governor that he had documented his policy six times between 1837 and 1855 in Western State's annual reports. He was confident that once the governor understood the policy, he would agree that it was a just and humane one.

Stribling invited the governor to visit Western State and personally inspect its various departments, which would better acquaint him with its policy. He concluded his letter by stating that, "Instead of constituting an institution where the afflicted would receive comfort and cure, any material deviation from their present policy would convert his hospital into one that was a bedlam, a mad house' indeed!"[3] The governor did not respond.[4]

Western State had become symptomatic of a national problem, and it appeared to some that insanity was growing while the solution to insanity remained elusive.

Meanwhile, at Eastern State, Galt was taking a different approach, perhaps because he believed that the rules that governed the sane also governed the insane. Consequently, patients presently in institutions, could function outside of them if they were in an environment that deviated as little as possible from their former family experiences. To support his view, in 1855, Galt wrote an article entitled "The Farm of St. Anne," wherein he described innovative experiments to cure the being conducted in Europe.[5] Galt certainly had not considered that some of the comments in his article would bring the wrath of his fellow superintendents down upon him.

A summary of his article follows. The Farm of St. Anne in France, wrote Galt, included facilities for insane patients and the farmer who supervised them. There, patients enjoyed the virtues of country life as they worked. If they had not been on the farm, they may otherwise have been confined to institutions, "that were little more than prisons such as those in New England, notwithstanding their internal comforts."[6]

Then Galt described an experiment at Gheel, Belgium where hundreds of insane persons lived and worked under the management of the villagers. He based his article on a paper written in 1852 by Dr. N.F. Cummings of England, who had described the Gheel experiment in detail. Patients there enjoyed almost unrestrained liberty and became useful members of the community. Cummings suggested that if America would implement similar systems, it might establish at least one new principle in the treatment of the insane.

> Those heading richly endowed asylums should consider the true interests of their charges instead of tinkering with pipes and studying architecture in order to erect costly, and at the same time, unsightly buildings. So far, America had done nothing.[7]

Galt's article caused a great furor among the superintendents that resulted in an extensive and serious discussion of his article at their next meeting. A summary of their remarks follows.

> Dr. Brown accused Galt of degrading the superintendents and their Accomplishments; he had "dishonored their fame. The animus that pervaded Galt's article was reflective of the man."[8]
>
> Dr Thomas. Kirkbride claimed that Galt slandered the men who managed hospitals in New England and misrepresented their institutions. He did not believe that mixing all colors and classes, as was done only in one or two institutions of the United States, was wanted in other hospitals.[9]
>
> Kirkbride further asserted that some superintendents, who had only a few chronic

demented cases, did not understand that restraints and restrictions were needed to control the movements and actions of the recent insane. Those who had visited Eastern State, where a great amount of freedom was allowed, knew that the relationships permitted between the patients and the townspeople were not seen in any other institution in the country.[10]

Dr. Nichols questioned why Galt's article referred specifically to institutions of the Northeast as appearing as "mere prison houses," when they were similar to those located in other regions. Several of the superintendents questioned the wisdom of The *American Journal of Insanity*, publishing his article, agreeing "that such wholesale libel should not have been published."[11]

Dr. Workman did not doubt that superintendents in New England had relieved human suffering; however, he disapproved of any attempt by the association to censure the American Journal of Insanity. The good qualities possessed by some of the superintendents were accompanied by a few amiable weaknesses. Their annual reports showed them to be abundantly short of perfection. Some of them seemed to be rather thin-skinned; and consequently, they winced under reproof.

As to the character of the buildings, little could be said in favor of their external beauty or internal arrangements. While in Worcester the day before, Workman had seen masons tearing down old strong rooms and cells and replacing them with rooms, sitting rooms and dormitories. Those changes indicated that progressive tendencies had finally reached New England, where they had been rather tardy.[12]

A few superintendents criticized Galt because he no longer attended association meetings and seldom visited other hospitals. Nor had he traveled to Europe to observe psychiatric practices there first hand. The superintendents also argued that Galt's decentralization proposals would reduce their hard-won power to directly control the destiny of their patients. The superintendents, however, did not oppose participation of laymen in hospital affairs; indeed, some wished to increase it. But they accused Galt of having gone too far seeking shared responsibility with the community for patient care; for example, boarding out patients.[13]

The superintendents responded formally to Galt's suggestions in the 1857-1858 edition of the American Journal of Insanity. They questioned permitting so much association between a person with a diseased mind with another patient with a similar illness, and they criticized placing insane patients in an environment that they believed had too much of a monastic character. Yet, the superintendents agreed that Galt was earnest, and his long experience added weight to his suggestions concerning an important subject. Since views similar to his had been warmly advocated in two Trans-Atlantic publications, the subject required more consideration than it had been given.[14] Privately, however, some of the superintendents felt that Galt received his just desserts from his critics.

The superintendents concluded that institutions where patients were treated as "senseless atoms," or subjected to daily routines similar to the monotonous motion of a machine, were far behind the spirit of the age. An institution should give every patient the greatest freedom that his mental condition would allow: curative and custodial occupation and amusements, and comfort and restoration. Any institution that did not meet these standards did not embody the principles of construction, organization, and management almost unanimously adopted by the profession.[15]

It is only conjecture to assume that the implementation

of Galt's suggestion could have reduced overcrowding in Virginia's hospitals and others in the nation. Another suggestion by Galt, if implemented, may have reduced administrative expenses. Should Virginia build a third hospital for the insane, Galt asked Stribling, would he support Galt's suggestion to confine males at Eastern State and females at Western State. Because Stribling believed that Dix understood the subject better than he did, he asked for her views on the matter.[16]

Later, Galt wrote an article entitled "On the Propriety of Admitting the Insane of Two Sexes into the Same Lunatic Asylum." A summary from it follows.

> Keeping the sexes strictly apart demanded ceaseless vigilance by the hospital's officers, who should be engaged in their important duties instead of such ridiculous and utterly useless activities. It was also difficult for the officers to mange a promiscuous crowd of male and female attendants.
>
> Intrigues of all sorts, perpetuated among the great numbers of male and female servants, caused more injury to the hospital than one who had not experienced them could imagine. Consequently, in many hospitals, such problems were not counterbalanced by advantages. Each hospital could accommodate more patients if their baths, apartments, gardens, and court wall were designed specifically for each sex.[17]

By the late 1850s, in a serious attempt to relieve overcrowding at Eastern and Western State, the Virginia legislature began to consider building a third hospital for the insane in western Virginia. Stribling's influence on its creation is revealed in his correspondence with Dorothea Dix who volunteered to support the project. While Stribling declined her offer, he acknowledged that at the proper time, her personal efforts in Richmond would be extremely valuable. However, it was not prudent to pursue the matter before the present legislature. His immediate objective was to first educate the public about the proposal, and then the members of the next session of the legislature, who would be considering it. After that, he would feel most grateful for her aid. He promised Dix that he would keep her informed of the hospital's progress so that she would know "when and where" to exert her influence.[18]

On July 23, 1858, Stribling reported to Dix again. He felt that the commissioners had made a fortunate selection of a site. The character of the land, its accessibility, and water advantages were unusual. The coal on the land, almost without cost of materials, would furnish fire and lights, a feature that no institution in the country could boast. He included in his letter an article from a Petersburg paper that would give Dix more information.

The hospital's directors, Stribling continued, who seemed cautious and deliberate, had asked Stribling for his suggestions and an endorsement of their plan for the buildings. Doubtless Dix would agree with him that they appoint a physician before taking any other steps. The board, however, was not prepared for his suggestion, and it might send the matter to Governor Wise for his advice. If Dix approved, a letter from her to Governor Wise might do much good! She should, if she wrote, "have to do so speedily as the governor was a 'quick' man."[19]

The directors had requested only that Stribling and Dr. Kirkbride review the plans, and because they did not visit the site, he and Kirkbride knew nothing personally of the land, and therefore had not alluded to it. However, the architect informed them that the building they had approved could not be located on the land presently owned by the institution. There was, however, adjacent land that the owner refused to sell. The directors considered applying to the next legislature for authority to have the land condemned, in order that they might obtain it.

Needless to say, the entire matter had attracted attention and inquiries. Stribling wondered why the original 300 acres the state already owned could not provide sufficient space for 250 patients. Now would be a good time for anyone opposing the location to do so. Stribling however, believed that it would be improper for him to volunteer any opinion. He fully agreed with Dix that it would be better for the state to lose $25,000 than to spend $200,000 or $250,000 to build an institution that, when completed, would fail in its humane goals.

A year later, Stribling wrote Dix to give her another update. As usual, he included some personal information. The rumor that Dix had heard, that on January 1 his annual salary would be raised to $3,500 was true. Stribling believed that he and other superintendents earned their salary if they faithfully discharged their duties.[20]

The Northwestern Hospital still was not complete when Virginia seceded from the Union in April of 1861. The western part of Virginia that refused to secede became the new state of West Virginia, an event that left Stribling with many patients who should be in the new hospital but still was unable to receive them. The West Virginia legislature renamed its hospital "The West Virginia Hospital for the Insane" and appointed Dr. James A. Hall as its first medical superintendent. Hall had gained his experience at the Pennsylvania Hospital for the Insane.[21] Later, a raid on the hospital by Confederate soldiers destroyed one ward and deprived all of the patients of their blankets, a forewarning of Sheridan's future vandalism at Western State in 1865.[22]

In 1865, the hospital's directors appointed Dr. Hills superintendent. In his first annual report, Hills wrote that construction had advanced to where he could admit twenty-one patients. Progress had been made even while West Virginia had been under pressure to establish its own existence. For both humane and economic reasons, Hills soon became a strong advocate for early treatment of the insane, thereby reinforcing views that Stribling and other superintendents had held for years.

"Blindness was incurable and the deaf mute could not be made to hear," wrote Hills, "but he thanked God that insanity was curable. Between one-third to three-fourths of the insane could be treated and then sent home to assume their responsibilities. For those treated early, sixty to eighty percent were restored. For those reasons, it was urgent to educate the public that insanity was as curable as most other diseases, for example, typhoid fever, pneumonia, dysentery, and scarlet fever, and it was much more curable that dyspepsia, consumption and small pox."

Hills concluded "it was cheaper to cure patients than to provide only custody for them. An *uncured* person was a dead weight upon the public, whether in or out of a hospital, and continued to be so as long as he lived. A *cured* person restored to reason in a few months was a burden only for that short period. One person not restored could therefore cost more than a dozen recovered cases. The expenditure of one dollar to cure one insane person would save ten to twenty dollars maintaining that incurable person through life." At that time, there were still one hundred patients from West Virginia at Western State and forty at Eastern State.[23]

Even though the West Virginia Hospital was completed, most state legislatures throughout the nation were unable to continue to provide limitless funds to erect enough buildings and hire people to accommodate the ever—increasing insane population. Legislators trying to solve the problems were faced with conflicting solutions offered by a variety of professionals. Pliny Earle, a respected superintendent of a hospital for the insane, asserted that insanity was becoming more and more an incurable disease.[24]

Then Dr. William Hammond of the New York Bellevue College questioned the credentials of some of the superintendents. Some of them, he believed, were ignorant of the anatomical roots of insanity; and consequently, they did not always provide the patients with proper medical or surgical therapy. Physicians treating other diseases were capable of treating insanity; and besides, sequestering patients in hospitals was often unnecessary and could be injurious to patients. Hammond also charged that for many years some superintendents had exaggerated the numbers of the recent insane that they could cure.[25]

After that, other respected superintendents began to make recommendations that did not favor incarceration. For example, Dr. Edward Jarvis and others recommended that those who were only mildly insane be treated at home.

Nationwide, by 1870, custody had replaced cure in most of the hospitals for the insane in the nation. Providing minimum care for the chronic insane left few resources to practice the tenets of moral medicine: early treatment, high attendant-patient ratios, effective classification, and availability of work suitable for patients.

Stribling and Dr. Hills believed that a policy not to treat curable patients was inhumane and also economically unsound. Therefore, Stribling, during his tenure, had used every means at his disposal to move his incurable patients elsewhere and not admit more of them. Society, he believed, would benefit each time he admitted a recently insane person, cured him, and sent him home where he could be productive. The cured patient's release thereby created a vacancy, and the process could be repeated.

It was not possible, however, to maintain Stribling's policies in Virginia or elsewhere, because hospitals for the insane had not been created only for the insane that could be cured. They also had been created for those who could not be cured. Other forces had also contributed to the demise of moral medicine. More of the insane had been placed in hospitals after 1850, not only because the insane were increasing along with the general population, but also because some superintendents suggested that insane persons could pose dangers to the general public: they might commit an atrocious acts or spread their madness like a contagious disease. Therefore, the public came to believe that insane persons must be placed into hospitals for their own safety.[26] Since moral medicine had always been considered a treatment for the recent insane who could be cured if they were in an environment where its tenets could be practiced, it was not viable in institutions where all of the patients were incurable. Thus, the reason for its demise.

The South had the additional problem of caring for insane blacks whose numbers were increasing at an alarming rate. The culture required the erection of separate institutions for them. In Virginia, once again, large numbers of insane persons who could be cured were not because its hospitals had no room for them. Also, fewer patients within the hospitals were being cured because scarce resources for curable patients were being shared with incurable ones.

Yet Stribling continued to believe that it was inhumane to allow those who could be cured to become chronically insane. He therefore continued to publicize the plight of those who could be cured. In the early 1870s, according to Stribling, 300 persons were being held in Virginia's county jails, almshouses, or just wandering about. Most of them were boarded at state expense.

His efforts included suggesting to the legislature that they consider efforts by officials at Eastern State Hospital to enlarge its hospital to accommodate one-hundred more patients, an act that would result in partially relieving the problem. He recommended that the legislature take action promptly, judiciously and efficiently to provide for its insane persons. Stribling reminded the legislators that Virginia had been the first to create a hospital exclusively for the insane and the first to build a hospital for insane blacks. He also wrote that similar institutions nationwide were in the same predicament. A number of them, according to Stribling, were enlarging their institutions by erecting some of their buildings in districts based on population and accessibility.[27]

Surely Stribling knew that he was fighting a battle that he could not win. For several years he had been forced to turn away patients that he was sure he could cure. By 1871, it must have saddened him that nearly all of his patients were incurable. Only eight of them were favored to recover, twenty-six others were doubtful, and the remaining three hundred and six patients was decidedly unfavorable.

As a result, Stribling wrote his directors, the situation at his hospital was depressing and dismal. He and his staff had to constantly draw on their skills, energies, and goodness of heart to soothe patients' depressed spirits and attempt to replace their delusions with pleasant thoughts. It would have been far easier for them to restore curable patients who would be in the hospital only for the brief duration of their illness. The present law, however, did not allow him to remove any of those patients to make room for those he could cure. Stribling predicted that he could cure seventy-five percent of the recently insane if he had room for them.[28] Although Stribling and his caretakers were dispirited, they still did not give up. During the winter of 1872, they tried to raise their patient's morale by presenting plays of light and humorous character. Those at the hospital responded favorably.[29]

Years later, in hindsight, it is easier to question past decisions that were made by superintendents and state legislatures. Could separate institutions for males and females have made a difference? Could more patients have been cured at less expense if, early on, different institutions had been erected for curable and incurable patients? Could the St. Anne and Gheel experiments in Europe been effective in the United States? At least, in some of those situations, data would have become available to legislators, allowing them to better analyze their allocation of funds.

CHAPTER 9

Treatment of Insane Blacks in Virginia

Many years before slavery became an issue in the nation, whites in Virginia had been concerned about the influence that free blacks might have on their slaves. They were especially wary of free blacks who were intelligent, honest, and worthy. As their numbers increased, many whites even considered them "evil." Members of the legislature decided that soon they must move free blacks elsewhere to distance them from slaves. In his annual report in 1850, Governor John B. Floyd described the situation. An abridgement of his statements follows.

> Free people of color occupied an anomalous position among Virginians.
>
> They had scarcely any of a free man's privileges, and less security than slaves, in whom they excited feelings of jealousy. At the same time, the whites regarded them with suspicion. There were among free blacks those who were intelligent, honest, and worthy. Probably for those reasons, the harsh measures that the legislature often proposed by those who felt the evils of the increasing numbers of these people, had not become law.
>
> All admitted that this population had grown to be

an evil, but few agreed on how to remedy it. To banish free blacks by a law of the land, without assisting them or providing for them, seemed harsh and cruel. Yet, to allow the mischief to grow greater was contrary to the dictates of wisdom and sound policy.

Then the governor suggested that money that the state appropriated by law to the Colonization Society be set apart to be expended in the following manner. When the board was satisfied that a free person of color had moved out of the state and purchased land, then give that person the same sum that the state would have been expended to transport him to Liberia. That policy would induce the better class of free blacks to settle themselves where the prejudices and jealousies they felt in Virginia did not exist. The governor also recommended a law, as punishment, to expatriate any free black that had been convicted of petty larceny.[1]

Naturally, the governor's remarks would have influenced attitudes of the white population in the state as well Stribling and Galt. After all, the governor and legislature controlled both hospitals.

In his 1841 report to his directors, Stribling included a table from the 1840 Census entitled "Statistics of Insanity in the United States" to defend slavery. The table listed the numbers of insane whites, free blacks, and slaves in each state and territory in the union along with their proportion to the total population. Stribling concluded from the report that slavery as an institution produced a positive mental effect because free blacks in non-slaveholding states often were more insane more than free blacks in the slave states. If the picture painted by those statistics was true, wrote Stribling "his abolition friends in the North should offer their sympathy and benevolence to the poor blacks in their own area, who must be in a state of physical and moral destitution, before

offering it to Southern institutions."[2] Details of the report
are contained in Appendix D.

Several other individuals and associations challenged
the statistics and conclusions contained in the report. Dr.
Edward Jarvis believed its conclusions to be "strange and
almost incredible," crediting his remarks to the *Philadelphia
Journal of Medical Science in 1844*. Nearly all its statements
referring to the disorders of the blacks were a mass of
errors and totally inaccurate. After analyzing the report in
1845, The American Statistical Society sent a petition to
Congress and requested that they disavow the report and
publish a corrected one. Then in May of 1846, the
Massachusetts Medical Society appointed a committee to
inquire into the report, and their findings completely
refuted the report.[3]

Meanwhile, for some time, slave owners in the eastern
part of the state had been pressuring Dr. Galt to admit their
insane slaves to Eastern State. He agreed with them, and
consequently, during the legislative session of 1845-1846,
his directors petitioned the legislature to allow Eastern State
to admit insane slaves as patients, if their owners paid for
their care. The legislature granted their request on January
16, 1846.[4] That law, however, contained a provision that
whites had priority in admission over slaves, a provision that
later forced Galt to discharge some slaves to make room for
whites. After October 1, 1856, he finally succumbed to
legislative and public concerns over mixing the races, and
refused to admit more slaves. Instead, he used the rooms
that slaves would have occupied for insane whites being held
in jails.[5]

More progress was made to provide for insane blacks in

1848 when Virginia's General Assembly asked Stribling and Galt if they could maintain and cure insane blacks in their hospitals. Should the superintendents do so, the legislature requested that they estimate the expense to accommodate them. If either hospital could not provide for them, it must create a plan for their separate accommodations.

Galt and his directors had construed the Virginia Act of 1841, and clauses in previous acts of a general nature, to apply to free black persons. Therefore, Eastern State had always ministered to the needs of all classes of insane persons, irrespective of color or social position. Consequently, free blacks had always been given the same rights to admission as whites.[6] Galt assured the legislature that his hospital could provide facilities for insane blacks with fewer funds than it would take to maintain them in jails. As a consequence, the legislature approved a new building at Eastern State that would include a section for insane black men and their black attendants. In 1850, the legislature passed an act appropriating $11,500 to erect a separate building to accommodate insane free blacks at Eastern State.[7]

Admitting blacks of either status lowered Eastern State's status in the eyes of nearly all of the nation's superintendents. Dr. Thomas Kirkbride of the Pennsylvania Hospital strongly criticized Galt because he believed that the mixing of colors and classes was not good practice. An exception to Kirkbride's opinion was expressed by Woodward of Worcester State Hospital, who believed that no harm could come to whites if their contacts with blacks were slight.[8]

For his part, Stribling contended that the construction of Western State's buildings made it utterly impractical to accommodate black patients. Even if it were possible, he thought it imprudent to place the two classes of unfortunates within one enclosure. The differences between them in habits, tastes, and disposition, he maintained, required that the arrangement and management of an institution for the blacks should differ from the one designed for whites. For those reasons, Stribling anticipated negative consequences to both classes if they were integrated.

Stribling suggested that instead, a separate building for blacks be constructed in the vicinity of one of the present hospitals, whose officers could care for both institutions. With the aid of a competent and experienced architect, Stribling prepared an outline for a plain, substantial brick building that would house sixty black patients and cost approximately $15,000. Stribling planned the structure so that it could be enlarged easily and at small comparative costs.

Details of the structure proposed by Stribling's proposal are given in the following excerpts.

> The institution should be located where the climate was agreeable to the health of Blacks, and as close as possible to where a majority of blacks in Virginia lived. It should be built on land that allowed it be easily ventilated and kept dry. Adequate water could be obtained from an elevated source in order to pipe it inexpensively to the attic and throughout the building.
>
> Since occupational activities were required for the patients, there needed to be at least two acres of land per patient that could be easily converted into gardens and cultivated. Cheap manure should be available and also a ready market for the products produced. The hospital should be located with a view to financial advantages. It would also be desirable to have the hospital located with a view to financial advantage. Hence, the institution should be located

in one of the cities or large towns of the Commonwealth.[9]

Stribling obviously wanted the hospital built as far away as possible from Staunton.

The superintendents respected Stribling and sometimes turned to him for advice. For example, after the government approved Dr. Charles Nichols's preliminary plans for the new Government Hospital in Washington, D.C., that Dorothea Dix had fought for several years, Nichols visited Staunton to obtain Stribling's advice on how the hospital could best care for the many insane blacks in the District of Columbia.

For years Virginia's legislature had done nothing for its insane blacks, explained Stribling, because he and Galt could not agree on what action to take. He had supported a separate institution for blacks while Galt had been in favor of admitting them into existing institutions, allowing those who were not violent to act as servants in white wards. Later, Nichols requested Congress to erect separate buildings for insane blacks and provide them the same care received by insane whites. In 1857, the government hospital began accepting insane black patients.[10]

Slave owners throughout Virginia had always hired out their excess slave labor as had Stribling. He assured minimal contact with his white patients by writing detailed instructions to his officers and his other employees as to how to use them. Attendants were to supervise those slaves who worked in the patients' buildings. Slaves, could however, take care of patients in the small, detached buildings when the attendants were not available.

Attendants were to ensure that slaves addressed patients

in a respectful manner, always using "master" or "sir." Slaves must never give directions to patients. Nor could they give patients medicine or nourishment, dress their blisters and sores, bathe or dress them, apply or remove restraints, or take patients to their rooms or on walks. They could not take presents from patients or make bargains with them.

Without assistance from patients, slaves scoured floors, scalded bedsteads, carried slop and water buckets, and emptied and cleaned chamber vessels. Under the direction of attendants, they made beds, swept or dry-rubbed floors, carried food from the kitchen, set the table, washed dishes, and cleaned knives, forks, and spoons. The housekeeper supervised two slaves named Phil and Eliza to be sure that they spent all of their time attending the dining room, pantry, and the stairway leading to the kitchen. Two others, Frederick and Charles, worked as messengers and waited on tables during meals. Other servants worked near the kitchen, the washhouse and the soap house.

Attendants or hospital officers had permission to apply the muff or wristband to any slave who engaged in bad behavior. In contrast, they were rewarded recreation in the evening after their work was done for good behavior. At 9:30 p.m. slaves had to return to their quarters. Also, any black children who were necessarily on the lot were to be kept at the servants' house and not permitted in the kitchen, washhouse, or the soap house. The steward generally oversaw the work of the hired slaves.[11]

Several times Stribling and his directors unsuccessfully attempted to convince the legislature to allow them to purchase slaves to use as servants. Officers, they argued, spent valuable time supervising untrained and unreliable slaves used as servants. They also had to spend a great deal of time teaching them the rules of the hospital. Even servants of excellent character had to be trained before they were efficient and trustworthy enough to have a positive effect on the patients.

Stribling became very impatient with slave owners who indulged their capricious slaves. As a result, those who became unhappy after being disciplined frequently were not forced by their owners to remain at the hospital. In addition, when contracts with the owners were reviewed at the end of the year, owners often exchanged slaves who had become more valuable, because the hospital had trained them, with others who were ignorant. That change necessitated a repetition of the entire training process. As a result, hospital officers were hesitant to discipline hired slaves even when it was necessary.[12]

Accommodations for slave servants became a concern to Stribling in 1846. They were, he wrote, living in quarters so crowded that their health was endangered. As a consequence, their owners charged the hospital more to rent them. Stribling suggested that if his directors obtained funds to erect a suitable building to accommodate the servants, the amounts the hospital was paying to the slave owners would decrease, which would eventually defray the building's expense.[13]

Only one example has surfaced of Stribling complimenting a slave, although he may have done so. An abridgement of his request in December, 1852, to purchase a slave, follows.

> Richard was twenty years old and assisted Mr. Wilson, the baker. He was very young when his parents began working at the asylum, and it could be said that Richard had been raised at the institution. Richard belonged to Dr. Edward Berkley and when he died, his executor planned to sell Richard for

$900. Although the price was high, Stribling reported that it would cost the hospital at least $80 to $100 to hire even an inexperienced slave to replace him. Stribling did not want to lose Richard because he helped the baker turn more than two barrels of flour into bread for patients every day. He was honest and could replace the baker, if the baker should ever leave.

The directors relented and obtained permission from the legislature to purchase Richard.[14] By 1860, Western State owned three slaves and hired nine others.[15]

The 1860 slave schedule lists the slaves that Stribling personally owned at that time: a sixty year old male, a fifty-seven year old female, a forty-five year old female and a fifty-nine year old male whom he hired out to Western State.[16]. It is not known what rent Stribling received. It also appears that Stribling and his wife felt affection for several black women who were their servants. However, it was not unusual for white families to consider their slaves as "family."

A page in the Stribling family bible lists their names, the names of their children, and the birth dates of some of them. Listed were Rachel and her daughter Harriet, with no birth date listed for Harriet. Rachel's other children were William, born in 1835; Lewis in 1837; Sally in 1839, and Lucy in 1844. Nancy and her child Elisa were listed with no birth date for Elisa. Peyton was born in 1843 and Thomas in 1845. Fanny's child Rebecca was born in 1845, Hannah in 1846, Sarah in 1847, Mary Elizabeth in 1849 and Fanny in 1852. Lucy's child, Rachel, was born in October 1858.[17]

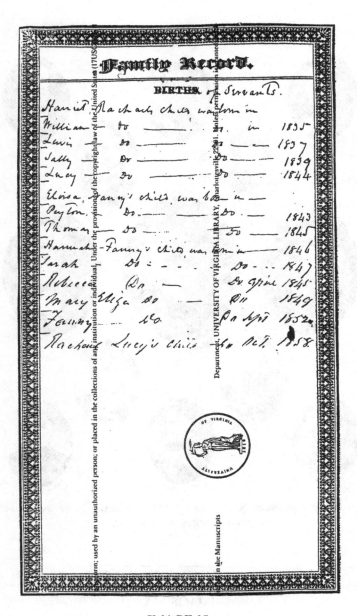

IMAGE 35

Page from Stribling Bible listing their female slaves
and names and birth dates of their children.
(Courtesy, University of Virginia Library.)

IMAGE 35A

The Thirteen Founders of the Association of
Superintendents of American Institutions for the Insane.
(Courtesy, Western State Hospital)

IMAGE 35B

The Virginia Institution for the Deaf and the Blind
Painted by Charles Wesley Bear
(Courtesy of the Virginia Institution for the
Deaf and the Blind)

An Analysis of the Patients at
Western State in 1860

The 1860 Federal Census provides an excellent window into the Western State Community near the beginning of the Civil War. Listed first was Dr. Francis Stribling as superintendent and chief physician. His name was followed by those of two associate physicians, a steward, seamstress, baker, domestic, nine male attendants, five female attendants, a night nurse, four male night watches (guards), and four female night watches, two firemen and a farmer. The 34 employees of the hospital cared for 372 patients. Given for each patient were his age, former occupation, marital status, place of birth, and illness. Details follow based on a statistical analysis of the data that refers to Western State.

There were approximately 219 male patients in the hospital. Ages for ten of them were unknown or not given. However, the youngest one was sixteen and two others were nineteen. Eighty-six of the males were in their twenties and thirties; 109 in their forties and fifties; 11 in their sixties, and one was 70. The marital status of 18 was unknown. One hundred thirty-two were single, 55 married, 12 widowed, and one divorced.

Although a majority of the men were born in Virginia, it was unknown where 7 were born. Sixteen were born in Ireland, 5 in Germany, 3 in Scotland, 3 in Prussia, and one each in England, France and Russia. Four were born in Kentucky, 3 in Pennsylvania, 3 in Maryland, and one in Ohio.

Former occupations of 22 of the male patients were unknown. However, 107 were laborers, farmers, or farmers' sons. There were 9 teachers, 7 clerks, 7 shoemakers, and 5 physicians. Other occupations included artists, blacksmiths, boatmen, cabinet makers, carpenters, clerks, coal diggers, cooks, coopers, confectioners, gardeners, gunsmiths, lawyers, merchants, millwrights, painters, peddlers, plasterers, saddlers, spinner's son, stonemasons, students, tailors, tanners, tobacco manufacturers, wagoners, wagon makers, wheelwrights and white smiths. So, nearly half of the men were laborers and farmers and the other men had been engaged in skilled activities or had been professionals, or engaged in business.

The illnesses of 73 of the male patients were unknown. Intemperance was listed for 25 and masturbation for 22. Eighteen had ill health; 10 epilepsy, 6 religious excitement; 5 fever, 5 blows on the head; and 5, excessive use of tobacco. Other patients had cerebral problems; concussions, convulsions; death of a family member; disappointment in love; domestic problems; dyspepsia; fright; palsy, Parkinson's; loss of business property or money and dissolute habits. At least 38 of the illnesses seemed to have been associated with physical problems.

At least 38 of the men's illnesses seemed to have been associated with physical problems. And many others today would be considered social and not moral problems.

There were approximately 153 female patients in the hospital. Their ages ranged from 15 to 70. Fifty-one were in their 20s and 30s; 71 in their 40s and 50s; and 17 in their 60s. The marital status of 5 of the women was unknown. Seventy-two were single, 61 married, and 14 widowed. Five of the females were born in Ireland, 4 in Germany, 3 in Prussia, and 2 in England. Three were born in Kentucky, 4 in Pennsylvania and one each in Massachusetts, Maryland, and North Carolina. Occupations of 17 female patients were listed as unknown.

However, two were teachers, 2 schoolmistresses, and 14 engaged in housework.

Forty of the females were listed as wives of farmers and laborers, and 6 as wives of physicians. Others were listed at wives of owners of apothecaries, blacksmiths, bricklayers, carpenters, clerks, clergymen, coopers, gunsmith, lawyers, merchants, millers, millwrights, saddlers, surgeons, tanners, teachers, and wagon masters. Eleven as daughters of farmers, 5 of physicians, 2 of laborers, one each of an apothecary, carpenter, and saddler.

The illnesses of 40 of the women were unknown. However, 16 suffered ill health, 11 domestic problems, 7 religious excitement, and 6 fever. Four were disappointed in love and 4 'death of a close family member.' Other ailments included childbirth, affliction, bodily injury, brain concussion, congenital problems, derangement, dyspepsia, dissolute habits, epilepsy, fright, masturbation, measles, mental suppression, nerves, pregnancy, religious perplexity, reversal of fortune, seduction, sedentary, and uterine problems. At least 30 of the females' illnesses seemed to be associated with physical problems.[18]

Some of their illnesses would not indicate insanity today. For years, the superintendents struggled to reach agreement on how to best define insanity.

In 1851, an article by Dr. Edward Jarvis was published in the *American Journal of Insanity*. It described how the differences in the temperaments of female and male patients affected their propensity to become insane. His article would have helped Stribling and his fellow superintendents better understand why their patients had become insane. An abridgement of his article follows.

Since there seems to be no functional difference of brain between the two sexes, we look to their temperament, character, or positions which have no relationship to the cerebral functions to see whether there is anything that leads to more insanity in one sex than the other.

Males have stronger passions and more powerful appetites than females who are more ardent, but less given to sensual indulgence. Male's inclinations and propensities, whether natural, intellectual, moral or physical, are more uncontrollable. More than female, males more often are overworked and disturbed in their brains.

Females are calmer and more patient; they endure difficulties and afflictions better than males, who are not as comfortable under trial. They yield sooner; being elastic, they recover quicker than males. Being firmer, males resist longer, and when they break down, they are unable to recover as quickly as females do under similar circumstances. Females' positions expose them less to causes of insanity such as changes in life and fortune, accidents and injuries.[19]

As a consequence of their habits, position, and exposure, males are more frequently intemperate. With more sexual passion and less sensibility, they are more given to masturbation and sensuality. Since men are more involved in business, more interested in property, politics, schemes of aggrandizement, and pursuit of knowledge, they more frequently become bankrupt, disappointed, and overwrought with labor and anxiety. Males are more employed with machinery and powder, and travel more frequently, sometimes to dangerous places. They are involved in strife's and bodily accidents, falls, and blows on the head more than females. The above factors cause more insanity in males than females.

Females are more sensitive, sympathetic, and affectionate. Therefore, they suffer more intensely from grief; loss of loved ones, ill friends, or causes peculiar to them. Females suffer from domestic problems such as ill treatment by intemperate or unkind husbands, children, or other relatives. Since females are more sedentary, more frequently dyspeptic, or more likely to have secondary irritations caused by their reproductive system, they suffer more ill health. Since females are more timid, they are more exposed to fright. Those causes were more likely to cause insanity in females than males.

Jarvis concluded "that males were more frequently attacked with insanity—that they are less curable when insane,—and that they more liable to death in their lunacy than females."[20]

It is unknown whether or not Stribling agreed with Jarvis but he did believe that marital status effected insanity in males, perhaps because he had observed that twice as many of his male patients were single than married. He wrote in 1841 that unmarried men were more likely to become insane than married ones, because they often gave "unbridled indulgence to their feelings, propensities, and passions of a depraved nature. Uninfluenced by the wholesome and purifying restraints of matrimony, some men plunged recklessly into dissipation and vice, reaping as their reward broken constitutions, ruined fortunes and reputations. They presented pitiable spectacles of minds in ruins."[21]

CHAPTER 10

The Civil War years

Until the war actually began, a majority of the people in Augusta County had favored maintaining the Union. After the attack on Fort Sumter, however, they wholeheartedly supported secession. Nothing in their recent past prepared them for what the war would bring or how long it would continue. Joseph Waddell, a Staunton historian, who kept a diary, recorded their trials and tribulations during that time in detail. Summaries from his diary follow.

There had been some military action in the town before the war started but soon it greatly increased. Hundreds of soldiers arrived and quickly departed while others remained longer. The military depot located there forwarded supplies to Confederate Army operations in northwest Virginia that depended on the supplies nearly entirely for their subsistence. By 1862, the depot contained enough clothing for ten thousand soldiers plus ammunition, cannon and other arms as well and ordinary quartermaster and commissary stores. A military staging center resulted in hundred of soldiers encamped in and around Staunton for varying amounts of time, as they were trained or waited to go to join their units.[1]

The first wounded soldiers arrived in early 1861, and for a time many of them lay on the floor of the sheriff's office and in the courthouse. The Confederate military soon placed 300 of them in the Institute for the Deaf, Dumb and Blind. Later they organized other hospitals in the area but they quickly overflowed.[2] By October 20, 1860, there were 1,000 soldiers in hospitals in Staunton and 250 more on their way. Staunton's citizens helped them any way they could. The wounded never stopped, some came to town on horseback, others walked, and as the war continued, many were barefooted.

One small group belonged to the Dunkard church that did not allow them to participate in the war. Some citizens were sympathetic to their plight.

Waddell remarked:

> There is something pitiful in the case of these people, flying, as they were to escape conscription, and being taken like partridges on the mountain. The whole crowd had a pocket pistol among them, and no other arms.[3]

In late September of 1862, five hundred prisoners captured at Winchester marched through town four abreast. One citizen remarked that it was pitiful to see so many human beings led or drive along like sheep. In June of 1863, 4,321 of them passed through, among them 45 women and children.[4]

The confusion was intensified by large numbers of wagon masters and teamsters with their animals and equipment that rushed into and out of the town. Train after train filled with stores and soldiers and stores arrived and departed from the train station. Soon they would be transporting the wounded away.[5]

In the midst of all of the confusion, apprehensive townspeople tried to maintain some semblance of their former life. Women sewed, knitted, cooked and nursed ill soldiers. Extreme devotion was shown by Margaret Crouse Haupe whose husband was a pharmacist. Her obituary in the *Staunton News Leader* on December 19, 1861 stated:

> The home of the deceased had been thronged by soldiers worn out and sick from the ordeals they endured. Her natural energy was stimulated beyond its ability in her constant ministrations to their wants, and she sunk under her cheerfully assumed tasks and died."[6]

As food and clothes became scarcer, depression and anxiety deepened among the people, and in time, some of them did not know where their next meal was coming from. Most of them became anxious when they heard constant dire rumors soon followed by even worse facts. Nearly all were sensitive to the death around them. Waddell, was walking from the cemetery in the morning of Sunday, January 4, 1863. As he passed by the grounds where the dead soldiers were buried, he noticed that the number of graves had increased since he was last there.

Waddell later wrote:

> It was almost appalling to see the rows of graves recently dug, waiting with gaping mouths for their still living victims. The sight brought before me vividly showed the sufferings of the soldiers dying in military hospitals, far from home and kindred, and all of the horrors of a time of war."[7]

The death of Generel Jackson devasted those in Staunton and others throughout the Confederacy. Waddell reacted by writing, "it was like the mourning in the Valley of Megiddon, when King Josiah was slain.[8] Even more trauma was on its way and this time it was more personal. Rampart rumors predicted a pending battle in the area. It gained credibility when Army hands began loading trains and wagons, ready to leave Staunton at a moment's warning.

On Sunday morning, June 5th, a battle began near the small village of Piedmont.

> From eight or nine in the morning until three in the afternoon, many citizens of Staunton were on the hills observing the smoke arising from the battlefield. For several hours not one of them imagined that a battle was in progreess only eleven or twelve miles away.

Army personnel and Staunton's citizens fled later in the afternoon, when they found out that Confederate General William E. "Grumble" Jones had been killed; his forces routed by General David Hunter. On Monday, June 6, 1864, Federal troops entered Staunton. One of the several Confederate soldiers who did not want to leave, remained there to capture a horse. When a Federal soldier drew near, he forced him to dismount, leaped onto the saddle and joined his command at Waynesboro.[9]

General Hunter met with the town people and agreed not to burn Staunton's workshops, if the citizens would pull them down, which they did. But early Tuesday morning, without notice, his soldiers commenced burning the buildings. They destroyed the railroad depot, steam mill, government workshops, Trotter's shops and stages, the woolen factory, Garber's mill, and the interior of the shoe factory. The Federal soldiers also released prisoners from the jail.[10] On

Wednesday, Generals George Crook and William W. Averill arrived and ordered their soldiers to search the town's houses. Even after the Federal troops were gone, the town remained quiet as though it was Sunday.

By June 18, the telegraph was up and running again between Richmond and Staunton.[11]

The *Richmond Times Dispatch* reported on October 10, 1864, that the *New York Herald* had published a letter from General Ulysses S. Grant to General Philip Sheridan, ordering him to burn every house in the Valley, destroy every mill, horse, cow, sheep and hog. Grant was determined to make the Valley a wilderness.[12]

Stribling and the other employees at Western State adapted to the war as best they could. Because the hospital was located at the intersection of the main two roads in the area, neither they nor their patients working outside could ignore it. Even though their hospital was somewhat self-sustaining, they still purchased some food and many other goods. Some eventually were nearly impossible to find. Stribling therefore instructed his employees to protect what supplies and resources they had. Laundry was not to be hung out at night to dry because someone might steal it.[13] Only Stribling, the steward, matron, or cook could permit cakes to be baked. Since loiterers distracted the baker, only persons transacting business there were allowed in the kitchen and they had to leave as soon as it was concluded.[14] Stribling also instructed his employees to conserve wood.[15]

Stribling emphasized to his employees that the health and comfort of the asylum's patients depended on the garden being managed skillfully. It was imperative to harvest the crops quickly and use food frugally. Only the gardener and his assistants could gather fruit. Stribling levied dollar fines against anyone who violated the rule.[16] The gardener was to record all of the fruit and vegetables that he distributed. Employees were not to sell, give away, or lend food unless the steward gave them permission to do so. The gardener was to give flowers daily, if possible, to the female attendants to distribute in their wards. He was not to send bouquets outside the hospital unless there was an excess of them after the inmates' hall had been properly supplied; and then, only with Stribling's permission.[17]

The stress on Stribling to provide for his patients during the war may have contributed to the physical breakdown that he suffered in March of 1863. He did not identify his disease but he told his directors that it was so obstinate and protracted, that for months he had been unable to even consult his officers on hospital affairs. His illness lasted until late that year and he was unsure whether he could be active and vigilant enough during the coming winter to do his job. Stribling's directors reported that, "he had been delayed by tedious and severe indisposition that for months prohibited his attention to business and recently compelled him to visit Richmond for medical and surgical assistance. Stribling returned to Staunton greatly improved."[18] Stribling later said that the hospital suffered little during his absence because his experienced and competent officers had adhered to the hospital's by-laws.

The apprehensions suffered by the Stribling family increased in April of 1864 when eighteen-year Frank enlisted in Chew's Battery at Gordonsville, Virginia.[19] Just six months later, he was captured by Federal troops and incarcerated at Point Lookout, Maryland. A nephew in Baltimore wrote to

Stribling's daughter Ella that, "Your brother Frank passed though Baltimore as a prisoner and he has been sent to Point Lookout. He seemed quite well."[20]

Dorothea Dix, who had become superintendent of Female Nurses of the Army in June, 1861, wrote to young Stribling when she learned that he had been captured.[21]

She wielded a great deal of power and influence during the war. Through her Washington office, she allocated large quantities of hospital supplies and obtained medical supplies from private sources when the government could not supply them. She not only carved out a role for women as nurses, but also influenced the public attitude toward them.[22]

Her letters to Frank indicate that Dix did not abandon the many friends she had made in the South during the years that she was there advocating humane treatment for the insane. Stribling responded to Dix on December 17, 1864. The following letters are presented in their entirety.

> Your note has just been handed me and I hasten to reply. I am much obliged for your kind offer to supply my wants. I am glad to be able to report myself quite comfortable and in want of nothing at present. Since my imprisonment I have suffered occasionally from dyspepsis—with that exception I am very well. I should like much to be able to receive a box of eatable, but no permits of any kind are being granted. The rations, altho quite sufficient, do not agree with me. If you could obtain a permit for me, I would be under lasting obligations. Should you have an opportunity of sending a letter to my parents, be so kind as to tell them where and how I am—that I wrote per last flag of truce in October and also put a personal in the New York Times a few weeks since. My cousin Mr. Spencer of Baltimore has kindly sent me money. If you can spare time from your arduous duties, I will be much pleased to hear from you again. Address as

above, care of Major A. G. Brady. Very respectfully
yours, F.T. Stribling, Jr.[23]

On January 17, 1865, Stribling wrote Dix again. By now
he was feeling the strains of imprisonment.

> Yours of the 21st of January has just been received.
> I was glad to hear from home tonight. Mrs. Stribling
> and I are much obliged to you for writing me. I
> received two letters from home by the last truce boat.
> I enclose you one. Since I last wrote you my health
> has not been good, although I have taken particular
> care of myself. My eyesight, which has always been
> very imperfect, has failed me much since my
> confinement. Presuming upon the intimacy existing
> between my father and yourself, may I not ask you to
> use your influence in getting me exchanged on one
> of the boats which are now running for that purpose.
> My constitution you remember has always been
> delicate. I fear nobody on myself but on my parents
> who are extremely anxious about me. Will you be so
> kind as to aid me? It would give me much pleasure to
> hear from you again. Be so kind as to give Mrs.
> Stribling my address and ask her to write me. Your
> friend truly, F.T. Stribling, Jr.[24]

Mrs. Henrietta Stribling wrote to her son Frank on
December 1, 1864. This is the only letter written by Mrs.
Stribling that has surfaced.

> Your letter, my dear child, was received about
> ten days ago. I was rejoiced once more to see your
> handwriting, telling me you were well. I am tolerably
> comfortable, and since then have seen Mr. B. who
> was exchanged. He told me that he left you and
> Ranson some little articles that he had collected for
> his comfort, such as a stove that I hope you may find
> useful to you as long as you stay.
> I trust in the course of events that you will soon be
> exchanged; your youth and delicate constitution will

no doubt be in your favor. I hope that you will observe all of the rules laid down for the prisoners and thus get on quietly. Mr. B said that you had a prospect of getting a place left by T. Hammond's exchange. I hope you did, as then you will have some employment and less exposure, as I understood it. R. Phillips tells me an exchanged prisoner brings the news of your being in the hospital sick, and that has made me anxious.

Write and tell me how you are. I heard you had a daily prayer meeting that I hope you enjoy and attend. For if we have access to our blessed Savior, we may be happy, even in captivity. The pleasures of the world are worth but little compared with the peace that our Father gives his trusting children for Christ's sake. My longing desire is to meet you in heaven and I see you walking and living very near to Jesus. For this and my daily prayers ascend, and we meet in spirit, often I hope. Sunday is our communion, and how I shall long to have you at my side. But before long, we shall, by the power of God, if you continue to love and serve him, sit down in our Father's kingdom.

Your friends and relations all are well. Fannie will move to Roanoke in a week or two. They have rented a house there for the winter. She was quite sick, and now is better. I sent Betsy to help her move and fix her house. Ella talks of going down after Christmas. I wish we could all be together then. Have you gotten letters from any of our friends in the North? Let us know. Your father is at the asylum all the time, with 300 of the insane to take care of. May the Lord reward his labors. Have you an overcoat? Let me know. We have written twice. Did you get the letters? Your dear mother.[25]

On March 4, 1865, Federal forces under Sheridan raided Western State. Stribling's description of the event is summarized below.

A detachment from General Sheridan's command made an assault upon the meat house, flour house, storeroom and other out buildings; bearing off and

destroying about 180 barrels of flour, 10,600 pounds
of bacon, 300 bushels of corn, a considerable quantity
of eggs, 135 bushes of rye and oats, 3 valuable mules,
wagons and carriage harness, 50 pairs of coarse shoes,
and many articles of wearing apparel from the laundry.

The hospital staff watched as the Federal troops
vandalized Western State and destroyed the precious
supplies. The action on the part of General Sheridan's
officers was not excusable under any pleas of military
of necessity.

The hospital suffered considerable financial loss.
Flour cost seven to ten dollars a barrel; bacon, twelve-
and-a-half cents a pound; and corn and rye, one dollar
a bushel, if they could be procured at all. Stribling
found the commanding officer and promptly
described his institution and the number of insane
patients under his care. He explained the difficulty
he had had obtaining the supplies and his fear that he
would be unable to replace them. His words fell on
deaf ears and the Union troops plundered the hospital.
Stribling took small gratification that the soldiers did
not enter the buildings occupied by patients. Union
privates showed more restraint than the officers.[26]

The experiences of Eastern State Hospital at Williamsburg
during the war were quite different from those of her sister hospital
in Staunton, especially for the patients. Expecting a Union invasion
in late April of 1862, Eastern State's directors and most of its
officers fled the hospital and the town.[27] When Union forces
reached the hospital, they found only Somerset Moore, a white
ward master attempting to care for 252 patients and only enough
food for them for supper.[28] A week or two later, Dr. John Minson
Galt died. Rumors as to the cause of his death still exist: Federal
troops kept him from entering his hospital, his concern for his
patients aggravated his medical problems, he accidentally
overdosed on laudanum, or deliberately used it to commit
suicide.[29] The truth has never been determined.

In 1863, Major General Foster asked Dr. John P. Gray, who was then in Williamsburg inspecting concerning another incident, to visit Eastern State and suggest how Foster could manage the hospital more efficiently, and make the patients there more comfortable.

Dr. Gray agreed to help, and after finishing his inspection, he sent his report to Major Foster who published it in the *New York Times* on October 31, 1864. A summary of that article follows. Gray wrote that Eastern State had spacious grounds and its commodious buildings that were reasonably well kept, clean, and in fair condition. Patients were well cared for and the hospital's environment was comfortable. The hospital's able physician, Dr. Weaver, had a good heart. Gray also praised the matron and other officers and their attendants who had discharged their duties with their only reward being food and clothing:

Servants cultivated a garden that yielded summer vegetables, and they obtained fish and oysters from the York River during season, The Union Government provided Army rations of fresh and salt beef, pork, flour, beans, rice, hominy, coffee, tea, sugar, potatoes, vegetables, dried fruit, salt, vinegar, soap and candles. It also supplied fuel, clothing, bedding, and furniture.[30]

The officers and soldiers carried out their duties in a spirit of charity. Colonel West told Gray that his soldiers possessed heartfelt sympathy for the patients and that they were willing to help them, although they were often unsure of what they should do. The *United States Sanitary Commission' in New York* [31] with its universal charity, furnished comforts beyond the reach of the Government, and a number of philanthropic persons from the North contributed both moral and material aid.

Gray concluded that, based on his personal interaction with officers and his observations of the hospital, he could verify Eastern State was being "conducted in a gentle and Christian spirit. That the United States authorities assumed the support of such an institution, and the military officers cheerfully took upon themselves the additional labors and anxieties necessarily incumbent, reflected the highest credit on the humanity and munificence of the Government and the character of its military."[32]

When the Union turned the hospital over to civilian authorities on October 31, 1865, it contained 180 patients, compared to some 250 in 1863. In his last entry on October 28, 1865, Surgeon P. Wager wrote that he had ordered medical supplies and everything else needed for the patients, except food, in amounts sufficient to last through the winter. Wager estimated that, because of the conditions of the road, the supplies might not arrive for ten days. There was no evidence that they ever arrived.

When Virginia's civilian board of directors took possession of the hospital on November 1, they challenged Wager's views. They reported to Governor Pierpont that the buildings were in a deplorable condition and the gas house was in such disrepair that it did not work. The patients' clothes were disgraceful, there was only enough food for one meal, and there were no funds left. Governor Pierpont released $15,000 to the board to take care of the immediate needs of the hospital, for which the board thanked him.[33]

An unbiased view of the hospital may have come from Dr. Hubbard, a frequent visitor there who said that he had never known the hospital to be in better condition than it was when it was under the administration of Wager.[34]

During the war, both sides vied for the honor of civilized behavior toward the patients, and treated them better than might have been expected. Although there were many crises, the hospital was provisioned during the war. Even at the first sign of danger, when most of the staff and board members were gone, a few persons, sometimes only one, remained to take aggressive actions to assure that the patients were fed.

CHAPTER 11

After the War

During the years immediately following the Civil War, Stribling faced one daunting challenge after another. One had been the loss of the former supportive Virginia legislature, and worries over how his hospital would be viewed by the Pierpont government. Also unsettling was whether or not, as a former official of the Confederacy, he would be allowed to keep his job. More personal was the loss of his slaves at a time when his wife's health was worsening and his own deteriorating. Equally troubling was losing control over the patient population occupying his hospital where, now, most of his patients were incurable.

Most others in the South were also apprehensive. The Civil War had left Virginia and the rest of the South in shambles: many of its rails torn up, factories destroyed, farms laid to waste, towns wrecked, and banks insolvent. For several days, after General Lee surrendered on April 15, 1865, Staunton and many parts of the South had no government, legal currency, mail, newspapers, or reliable communication with the outside world. Understandably, all were troubled and anxious about their future. Eventually, normalcy returned to Staunton only after Federal troops occupied the South in order to reconstruct it.[1]

Soon after the war ended, Union troops arrived in Staunton.[2] On May 8, a group of concerned citizens, attempting to determine their fate, met with Brigadier-General Duval. He informed them that he had no instructions regarding civil government and was in Staunton only to suppress guerilla parties and parole Confederate soldiers. During the remainder of 1865, citizens finally were able to hold elections.[3] Troops would, however, remain in Staunton until January 12, 1866.[4] Young Frank had been exchanged and paroled in Staunton in May of 1865. In the fall, he attended the 1865-66 session at the University of Virginia and returned to Staunton to work as a pharmacist.[5]

As a social being, Stribling surely had missed the fellowship and support of his superintendent friends in the North. There can be no doubt that he was happy to travel North to give a speech at their annual meeting on June 23,1868. The *Enquirer and Examiner* newspaper described his speech as brief but excellent, and printed it in its entirety. They also noted that Stribling was the only representative there from the unreconstructed states. Other superintendents wrote that they could not attend as they were on the eve of being removed from their positions, because the United States government had not yet pardoned them. (Neither had Stribling.) The Association attempted to support them by forming a committee to petition Congress to remove their disabilities.

Stribling's unedited speech follows.

If, gentlemen, any unkind feeling may have been engendered by the sectional strifes of the past, it is delightful to perceive that such have been dismissed from our minds and hearts. The unhappy controversy, which for four heavy years, divided and distracted the country having ceased, it is the duty of all good citizens to endeavor to blot out as far as may be practicable all bitter memories."

This is especially incumbent on an association like ours. Dedicated as our lives have been to one of the noblest of Christian charities, the acerbates of partisan politics can receive no countenance from the members of this association.

Called to minister to minds diseased, it would be strange indeed, if we could so far forget our appropriate office as to stimulate those vile passions, which have driven a nation to frenzy. On the contrary, let us bring our united efforts to the task of soothing popular excitement, of pouring oil on the troubled waters, and of inculcating 'peace on earth and good will towards men.'"

This is our appropriate mission. Nations, like individuals, are subject to paroxysms of insanity; and nations, like individuals, require a judicious system of moral treatment; and while we may not feel justified in taking charge of the nation and prescribing those remedies which are necessary to restore the national mind to a healthy condition, we can at least so employ the limited means at our command as not to aggravate the malady."

We can give expression to sentiments of charity, and teach the necessity for mutual forbearance. We can in our persons set examples of forgetfulness and forgiveness of injuries, real or imaginary. We can cherish among ourselves feelings of mutual friendship and regard, and when we return to our respective spheres of duty, we can carry back with us pleasant memories of our social intercourse, a more catholic spirit of nationality, and a more earnest purpose so far in us lies to restore fraternal feelings to our lately dismembered country."

Stribling's remarks were received by the association with applause, and its members directed

that his speech should be a part of their records, as
well as how it had been received by its members.[6]

Only Congress could remove Stribling's political disability,
and it was his responsibility to initiate the process by filing a
petition to them. Then Congress would consider Stribling's
petition along hundreds of others from former Confederates
in similar situations. Congress would then pass a Bill that
included the names of those pardoned.

Probably because of pride and economics, Stribling fought
to keep his position, although he may not have relished having
to fight to retain it. But Stribling's assets, ones that he had
worked for instead of inheriting, had greatly decreased during
the war, as they had for nearly everyone else in the defeated
South. It is also probable that Henrietta Stribling's health
deteriorated during those years, and Stribling no longer had
slave labor to care for her and maintain his household.

But Stribling was extremely fortunate that his brother-in-
law, John C. Bowyer had lived in Washington for many years
and knew many influential politicians there. It was Bowyer
who would champion and coordinate efforts to have Stribling's
disability lifted. Bowyer believed that the process should begin
as soon as possible because there were many others in Virginia
who would like to be superintendent of Western State Hospital.

Bowyer was pleased to write Stribling in February of 1869,
that Stuart of Nevada would report favorably on his petition.
His views of Washington at that time, as a defeated civilian
southerner, follow.

> Politics were even more rampant in Washington
> than usual because they were living in an age of
> falsehood. Bowyer did not believe anything that he
> heard, and scarcely anything that he saw with his own

eyes. To earn a living, he had been forced to keep
boarders, an agonizing business. Consequently, his
house was filled with generals,
     Colonels and subordinates from both branches of
the Federal military. Bowyer was especially bitter
that General Hunter was displaying, in his Washington
home, finery that formerly had been the property of
Southerners.[7]

Opposition to Stribling's petition came from E. H. Smith
who wrote to General Butler on February 1, 1869. "Stribling
and Judge Meredith of the Richmond Circuit Court had never
supported reconstruction or been sympathetic to Republican
men or measures. Smith continued that both men should
resign their lucrative offices that were being held in defiance
of the 14th Amendment. It was Smith's duty, as a loyal man
and a Republican citizen, to make the case against them."[8]

When Judge Meredith learned of Smith's letter, he wrote
Stribling that Smith had attacked him because he was Smith's
personal enemy, and Smith probably attacked Stribling because
he wanted his job. Meredith warned Stribling if Smith knew
that they were aware of his letter, he might persuade others
to give false affidavits to support his claims.[9]

Stribling, meanwhile, had a supporter in Alfred Chapman
of Alexandria who defended him in a March 9, 1869 letter.
He believed that Congress would pass the bill presently being
considered but, only after they amended it to exclude men
who were in the Confederacy in 1861, and military and naval
officers who had supported the South.[10]

During the first session of the Forty-first Congress in
1869, under 'Private Acts,' legal and political disabilities were
removed from large numbers of individuals in the South,
including Dr. Stribling and Judge Meredith.[11]

During that same time, Stribling and directors wrote their first annual report to the Pierpont Government. It was important to them that the Reconstruction Legislature understood Western State's history, including its accomplishments and future goals. They began by writing that "because of the abnormal condition of the government of Virginia, and its interruption during the past eight years, they were making a more detailed report than usual. They also hoped that the people of Virginia were being restored to their ancient relations to the Federal Union, and soon would enjoy the blessings of a government administered by their own chosen representatives. An edited version of their report follows.

Western State compared favorably with similar institutions in the United States in percentage of cures and cost per capita of maintaining its inmates. Since 1845, they and Stribling had several times suggested that the legislature address the needs of insane blacks. The white population in the West, however, had been averse to being taxed for the benefit of the slaves and slave-owners of the East. For that reason and a lack of funds their entreaties had been futile. Now that the former slaves were citizens, and entitled to a ratable participation from public revenues, it was imperative that the government provide adequately for them.[12]

Then the directors described activities that were presently available to Western State's patients as well as recent improvements to its buildings. The new reservoir had been completed, the steam department improved, the entire tin roof painted, and some new floors laid.[13] To improve the female patients' health, a spacious airing court was created and enclosed with a substantial brick wall. In addition, neat summerhouses had been erected, windows and locks improved, new bedsteads and wash stands supplied, and an "European" cooking stove purchased. It was to Stribling's credit that his powers of persuasion had allowed him to obtain funds for so many projects at a time when they were scarce.[14]

Stribling's efforts to attend the superintendents meeting a year earlier perhaps had unintended benefits. Although, they usually had their annual meetings in places with large populations, they chose the small town of Staunton for their 1869 meeting. Eminent physicians attended from almost every state in the Union as well as Canada. Their decision may have been affected by their high esteem for Stribling and their desire to restore kind relations with the superintendents in the South.

While in Staunton, they toured Western State Hospital, The Hospital for the Deaf, Dumb and Blind, and spent a day at Weyer's Cave. One evening while they were in Staunton, Stribling entertained them in his home. After their visit, the superintendents formally stated how much they enjoyed their visit, and thanked those associated with it, including the citizens of Staunton, for their hospitality.[15]

Because Western State had not been as adversely affected by the war compared to many other institutions, it stabilized sooner. Obviously, the stress felt by Stribling during that time diminished, even though resources remained scarce for some time. Now his challenge was to deal with a larger patient population with fewer employees. Therefore, he reviewed and revised existing instructions and created new ones. Descriptions of a few of them are summarized below.

Stribling forbade patients and others to gather at the medical office. Only attendants were to remove medicine cups, an hour before mealtime, and they were to give the medicine to their patients before they ate. Afterwards, the attendants were to return the empty cups to the office. An attendant could never remove another attendant's medicine without special permission, and must never leave medicines where patients might access them.[16]

Watchmen were to continue to protect patients and the hospital grounds from invasion by cattle, hogs, dogs, or other animals. They were to lock the hospital gates at ten o'clock every night.[17] To assure that female patients were protected, Stribling issued instructions that only physicians, the steward, and maintenance workers were allowed into their quarters. Even then they had to give timely notice to the matron before working there. However, Stribling allowed gentlemen to visit the hospital in the company of ladies or under authorized tours, and female attendants could receive male friends in the Center building.[18]

Protecting the hospital's grounds from encroachment became an issue in 1872 when a 100-acre tract of nearby land came up for sale. Stribling quickly recommended that the directors buy it. If anyone else obtained the land, he pointed out, they might divide it into small lots and then sell them to a class of people who would prove to be unsuitable neighbors. With improvements, Stribling believed that he could raise grain on the property, and as usual, his directors agreed with him.[19]

The ability of Western State to care for its patients during the war was mostly due to efforts by its caretakers and other hospital employees. Stribling decided to reward some of them when he lifted the ban on smoking. He instructed the steward to give moderate chews of tobacco to men working in the garden, on the farm, about the grounds, or in the laundry, steam, and gas works.[20] Stribling had been slower to embrace another suggestion that he probably believed was more extreme. Finally, however, his officers and attendants convinced him, as an experiment, to allow a dancing party once a week. Stribling wrote that male and female attendants who could be spared from their work could attend, as well as families of resident employees, if the attendants agreed to be responsible for them. The hospital provided suitable music and simple refreshments, and recorded those who danced. Male and female patients or attendants could not dance as partners; however, after the patients stopped dancing at nine p.m., officers and attendants could unite in a round dance.[21]

Stribling, the eternal optimist, never gave up. In early July of 1874, he determined to find out exactly how many insane persons in Virginia were living at home. Believing that Census records were incorrect, Stribling prepared his own survey. He created a form and a letter that he planned to send to all of the physicians in Virginia, because it was they who would know where families were that included an insane member.

Stribling requested that the physicians name any insane person they found because he did not want to count anyone more than once. As he did not want to hurt the feelings of any of the patients, or violate the professional confidence between them and their doctors, Stribling pledged that he would not divulge any of the names. He urged the physicians to promptly send him the information that he requested and also to use their personal influence to persuade other physicians to do the same.

Later, Western State's directors continued that effort.

Twenty-one counties in Virginia had not responded by the time that the directors wrote their 1874 report. Those who did, however, revealed that there were 491 insane persons living at home, in county jails, almshouses, or boarded out and paid for by the State. Others just wandered throughout the countryside.[22]

When Dr. Stribling became ill in the summer of 1874, his family and friends hoped that he would soon recover, but he did not encourage them. He died on July 23, 1874. Excerpts from an obituary in a Staunton newspaper describe Stribling's funeral.

Staunton mourned the death of one of its most prominent citizens. The town's merchants closed their businesses while the funeral took place.

> The funeral was large and well attended. All of the member of the Directors of the hospital living in the area attended, as did some fifty convalescent patients from the hospital. Several distinguished men of Virginia were among the pallbearers.[23]

Memorials to Stribling revealed personal information that did not surface elsewhere: his love for his family and friends, and his support of his church. Summaries from a few of them follow.

The Richmond Inquirer: No man in any field of usefulness won higher distinction than this lamented Christian gentleman whose death is not only mourned by his fellow citizens but through the limits of the land. What Maury and Lee were in their respective department, Dr. Stribling was in his. Each won undying glory for his own name and luster to the name of the old Commonwealth that they all loved so deeply and served so faithfully.[24]

The Southern Churchman: Dr. Stribling was learned in his profession, eminently skillful in its practice, and endowed with almost intuitive sagacity in tracing the cause of insanity. He discarded the harsh idea that the insane were, in some sort, accursed of God and proper subjects of severe and sometimes cruel discipline and torturing restraints. His work caused the spirit of love to breathe over chaos in order to bring order out of confusion. Stribling "was full of overflowing sympathy and tenderness of feeling, yet cool, deliberate and immovable as a rock when duty was to be done."

His patience never grew weary and his love never grew cold. He cared for the 'trifles that make the sum of human things' as well as the great things that surrounded him. He considered nothing unimportant that concerned the good order and success of his institution, he dispensed charities noiselessly as the silent falling of the dew.[25]

The Board of Directors of Western State Hospital: With a mind vigorous and comprehensive enough to embrace every great interest of the asylum, Stribling possessed the faculty of attending to every detail of its management. His perception was almost intuitive, and his judgment was rarely at fault. Possessing great equanimity of temper, he was always calm, patient and forbearing; and while he governed with a firm hand, the charm of his manner divested authority of all semblance of harshness.[26]

Alexander, Virginia: We speak of men as great, who are only great in destroying human life and human happiness. But here was a Christian man, who devoted all the powers of his body and the faculties of his mind, to minister to one of the most distressing and painful ailments to which human beings are exposed. While he was firm, he was as kind and gentle as a mother. His success was so great that other institutions followed his example, and at the time of his death, Western State was second to no other similar institution in the country.[27]

An Unidentified Friend: I have never known one who combined more of the elements of true greatness. Without thinking it a hardship, he sacrificed his comfort and convenience for the pleasure and well being of others, even those very young or very humble. Naturally genial, his life of heavy responsibility never subdued the cheerful vein of mirth, which was a prominent trait of his disposition. Nor did it ever render him irritable or impatient. So uniformly urban and serene was his temper, that I do not believe he was never known to be angry with anyone, child or servant. He was a kind, generous, sympathizing life-long friend; a gentle, indulgent father; a tender, solicitous loving husband, and a humble, consistent Christian.[28]

Under his hand, everything was so perfect in its working that even today, as city church bells toll for his funeral, that immense asylum with its hundreds of patients and officers and attendants is moving with the regularity of clock-work, while the master hand that set all in motion, is lying cold in death. However, his work was not accomplished without sacrifice and the severe physical and mental strain that it entailed.

Several times Stribling tried to resign from his position, but entreaties from many in Virginia caused him to remain.[29]

Trinity Episcopal Church: While others may speak of the great void that his death leaves in the scientific world, and of the irreparable loss to society and humanity; we, his friends and brethren, express our warm, personal and loving regard

for him as a man, a counselor, and a Christian. He has been
with us many years and sorely shall we miss his courtesy, his
scrupulous devotion to the true and the right, his Christian
temper, his earnest zeal for the church he loved so well, and
his conscientiousness in discharging every duty of his office.
We feel sorrow for ourselves when we think we shall see his
face no more in our midst.[30]

Gordonsville Gazette: Hundreds of afflicted ones under
Stribling's care showed the measure of their love, affection
and admiration for Stribling who was at once their Custodian
and their Liberator.[31]

The Vindicator (in Staunton): Stribling was more widely
known than any other physician for the insane in this country.
He discarded the practice of chaining patients and treating them
severely. His perception of his patients, the nature of their
insanity, and his ability to use all of the means he possessed to
cure them, gave him great success. Although firm, he was
gracious and gained the affection of his patients.[32]

Of Stribling's professional character, the celebrated Dr.
Kirkbride of Philadelphia, lately said that, "Stribing stands at
the head of his profession in America."[33]

Valley-Virginian: Stribling was so gentle and kind in his
intercourse with his patients, that they loved him with an
ardor and devotion seldom, if ever, exhibited by any class of
persons to another. He never met one of them without a
pleasant smile or word. In his intercourse with others, rich
and poor, he was a gentleman, acting on the principle that
politeness and urbanity cost nothing.[34]

Henrietta Stribling died in 1889. Her obituary read, "Mrs.
Henrietta F. Stribling, relict of the late distinguished Dr.
Francis T. Stribling died at her residence, No. 10 Market

Street, yesterday morning at 3 o'clock in her 76th year. She was a Miss Cuthbert of Norfolk. A large portion of her life she had been an invalid. She was one of the oldest members of Trinity Church and her Christian character shone in all the relations of life."[35]

In a speech in 1967, Doctor Hobart G. Hansen, who was then superintendent of Western State said, "Dr. Stribling created a golden age at Western State. He had no tranquilizers, no shock treatment, and knew nothing of psychoanalysis. Yet, out of his simple humanness, he had remarkable success in rehabilitation of the insane. Western State is still not the therapeutic community it was at the time of Stribling's death."[36]

CHAPTER 12

Western State Today

Western State Hospital has been in existence as a hospital for the mentally ill since it opened in 1828. Most of the buildings that were erected during Stribling's tenure still stand at the original site. Many of them are examples of Thomas Jefferson's architectural principles and several are on the National Register of Historic Places.

In 1976 the final patient was transferred to Western State's present site that is located east of Staunton off Richmond Road. Although it contains two dozen buildings, some are not presently being used. The hospital has its own doctors, nurses, maintenance staff and police. The staff serves thirteen community service boards in Virginia and admits and discharges patients from them. New treatments allow patients to quickly return to normal life.

During the move from the old site to the new one, concerned hospital employees moved hundreds of items. Among them are historic pieces of furniture that were placed in offices throughout the hospital. Plain, practical furniture made and used by the patients also was moved. Other items are stored in the archives or in other building on the site.

Among them are furniture, dish and glassware, kitchen equipment and farm equipment, restraint devices, medical equipment, pictures, paintings, photographs, all of the books from the library and much more. Also moved was an enormous quantity of archival material that describes in detail the hospital's history from its creation until the present time. Numerous historic medical books are also located there as well as Stribling's letters including his correspondence with Dorothea Dix.

After the move, Western State's old site was used as a prison by Virginia's Correction Department the property near the end of 2002. Since possible plans for its future have been examined, however, the property's size and restrictions as a historic property limits its use, and a public-private partnership may become necessary. Nevertheless, in 2003, the State of Virginia agreed to allow the City of Staunton to market the property and they are negotiating with prospective developers. The building directly behind the administrative one contains the beautiful historic chapel, and within its crumbing walls still stands the organ that W.W. Corcoran gave the hospital in the early 1852.

An important goal is that representative historic artifacts and documents be returned to the historic buildings and grounds so that they can be accessible to the hundreds of Virginians whose relatives were patients there, families whose relatives were employees, and historians. Surely, the site will attract visitors and historians nationwide.

EPILOGUE

D r. Francis T. Stribling was the first graduate of the University of Virginia's Medical school; the second superintendent of Western State Hospital for thirty-eight years; the author of a substantial revision to the Virginia state law governing the diagnosis and care of the insane; a long-time friend and advisor to social reformer Dorothea Dix; one of the thirteen founders of the association that later evolved into the American Psychiatric Association; and one of the earliest and most influential proponents of Moral Medicine in the American South.

He had a positive influence on the lives of thousands of insane Virginians and others. At a time when every institution for the insane in the South, and all but a few in the remainder of the country, were little more than penitentiaries, Stribling recognized that insanity was a disease, that if properly treated, was curable. His system of moral treatment was a distinct advance on everything in use at that time.

Dr. Robert Hansen, superintendent of Western State Hospital, wrote in 1967, "In an age of the common man, Dr. Stribling possessed an uncommon and profound knowledge of human nature, and the importance of human relationships. He believed that the drives, interests, and needs of the insane were the same as those of others, and that satisfaction of them through human relationships, would help restore their reason."

Throughout his tenure at Western State, regardless of the political consequences, Stribling challenged anyone, including the governor of Virginia, when doing so helped cure the insane.

For example, when Stribling wrote his first report to his directors in 1836, he stated that Virginia should be mortified that it was not curing its insane patients. Still, he soon won them over and they provided funds that Stribling requested to practice moral medicine. Its most important tenets were early treatment, nutritious food, work, exercise, amusements, and religious services. He specifically instructed his employees how to engage in efforts that would increase patients' self-esteem, especially being their friend, and he used restraints sparingly.

In the early 1840s, a bitter dispute arose between Stribling and Eastern State over Stribling's when Eastern State claimed that Stribling's admission policy was detrimental to them. It was to Stribling's benefit that already impressed the legislature with his annual report and personal interactions with individual members. That dispute confirmed that Stribling would be as political as he needed to be to achieve his goals.

The reputations of Stribling and his directors were not enhanced in 1852 by the way they defended themselves against charges that they abused their patients. By their own admission, their investigation that resulted, was rushed, and consequently, incomplete. Stribling's greatest offense was not deposing patients, thereby betraying his own assertions that nearly all of them understood right from wrong.

Stribling managed to provide for his patients during the Civil War, even after Sheridan's troops sacked his hospital. Although he sometimes disparaged free blacks, it was largely due to his efforts that Central State Hospital for blacks was erected. He was also involved in the creation of what would become the West Virginia Hospital for the Insane and the Government Hospital for the Insane in Washington. Because of his intense friendship with Dorothea Dix, he also influenced her efforts to establish numerous hospitals for the insane in the South. Stribling also gave an impressive reconciliation speech to the superintendents association in Boston in 1869.

In balance, because of his crusade to cure the insane, Stribling was one of the most influential Virginians of his time.

APPENDIX A

Instructions to Western State employees

Insight to the daily life of all of those at Western State can be obtained by reading the instructions that Stribling wrote to his staff, those in supervisory positions, other caretakers, patients, and servants. They also reveal the sacrifices that Stribling expected from his employees, many of whom were expected to spend nearly all of their time at the hospital. Stribling also used instructions to create an orderly environment at the hospital that reassured his patients. Initially they were contained in a "Regulation" book that was eventually replaced by the formal "By Laws of Western State."

Stribling began writing them in 1852 after the patient population increased, causing a proportional increase in employees. Over the years, he wrote additional instructions and updated existing. As a result, employees knew exactly where they should be and exactly what they should be doing each hour of the day. All employees involved with hospital property of any kind had to record their transactions at the end of the day. A summary of some of his instructions follows.

The assistant physician, steward, matron, and head of the clothes department were to spend all of their time at the hospital because of their wide and varied responsibilities. They were to assure that attendants treated their patients kindly and properly by keeping them safe, warm, and their areas clean and well ventilated. The steward made certain that the employees reporting to him followed hospital's rules and that patients' food was properly served and distributed. They also were expected to spend as much time as practicable with their patients.

The assistant physician accompanied Stribling on his daily visits to ill patients and other times as necessary. He prepared and stored medicines, and saw that the patients received them. The assistant physician supervised the male patients' bathing and their exercise and amusements. He exerted moral influence on the patients to further Stribling's views on their moral and medical treatment. When the steward was not available, the assistant physician received visitors and he was responsible for them while they were at the hospital.[1]

The steward was indispensable to the hospital's routine operations. With advice from the superintendent, he hired attendants, negotiated their wages, and reported those who were unfaithful, negligent, or incompetent. He was also responsible for the conduct of the servants. The steward purchased all items required by the hospital and insisted that they were used economically. He kept exact records of receipts and expenses, opened the buildings each morning, and made certain that the attendants and servants were up and engaged in their duties. Each evening, the steward closed the buildings and assured that employees and patients retired at the proper time. He also was the hospital's contact with the directors on a daily, monthly, and quarterly basis. In addition, he received visitors, supervised their tours, and answered their questions.[2]

The matron assisted the steward in his duties and had the primary responsibility for female patients. She also supervised the nurses and servants, directed the labor of female patients, and supervised their amusements. The matron recorded the movement of all items from one department to another, and as necessary, purchased articles for female patients in Staunton.

Because the night watchman protected those at the hospital and its grounds, Stribling, the assistant physician, and steward were available to him all times. Each night he made several rounds, quietly passing through areas containing sleeping patients, concentrating on those occupied by female patients. He made certain that attendants and servants were in place, and patients were quiet, comfortable, and safe. The night watchman also examined area that contained the wash house, and detached buildings occupied by servants. At least once each night, at an irregular time, he satisfied himself that those areas were orderly and only persons authorized by the steward were there.

The night watchman frequently visited the reservoir and walked along the line of pipe to the spring to ascertain there was no deficiency of water in the former, or leakage in the latter. He created procedures to follow if a fire occurred, maintained the hose, ladders, fire plugs, screw taps and other apparatus provided for the fire department, and assured they were accessible, even should he be absent. Monthly, the night watchmen held practice sessions with the members of the Fire Company. Under his direction they practiced attaching the hose to fire plugs, moving reels rapidly to distant points, and adjusting ladders. When he was not occupied in other duties, as directed by the assistant physician, he took charge of some patients and provided them exercise or amusement.[3]

The performance of the gardener was important to assure that the self-sufficiency achieved with the garden continued to be maintained. Each morning, he went to the male wards and took charge of patients who would be working for him that day. He disbursed them in the garden, orchards, or on the grounds surrounding the main building. He understood that Stribling expected him to treat them kindly, and prevent them from escaping. The gardener also worked with his hired hands, advised the steward what to purchase and received items. In the summer, each day if possible, he sent flowers to female attendants who distributed them to the various wards.

The gardener understood that he could not sell, loan or give away products from the garden except by permission of the steward. However small the amount, the matron could find a patient or patients who would enjoy and benefit from it. He recommended to the steward any excess bouquets that could be sent from the institution, but only with permission of the superintendent. Near the end of the day, the gardener asked the matron the quantity of vegetables that she would need for the next day.[4]

Assisting the gardener was the hospital's farmer who supervised the patients and hired hands as they planted and harvested crops, built and maintained fences and gates, maintained farm equipment, and cared for the cattle, horses and hogs. In the late fall and early winter, he supervised all activities pertaining to butchering animals. If the steward sold or loaned any article to someone outside of the hospital, the farmer delivered and recorded it. He also credited returned items to the proper account. The farmer also recorded salaries for hired hands and expenses for blacksmithing.[5]

APPENDIX B

Superintendents Discuss Restraints

Superintendents throughout the nation were faced with restraint problems similar to those discussed by Stribling. A growing insane population further overcrowded hospitals and without increased funding, many superintendents believed that they had no choice but to use more restraints. In 1859, Dr. J. J. McIlhenny addressed restraints in his paper entitled, *The Various Means of Restraints for the Violently Insane.*[1] An abridgement of an in-depth discussion by a group of superintendent's follows.

McIlhenny believed that caretakers should not engage in activities that gave a sensitive patient ideas of tyranny and oppression. Over the past year, with 277 patients, he had used restraints only four times, for extreme cases and for as short a time as possible. They consisted of muffs, gloves, and camisoles. Instead, McIlhenny lined two or three plastered rooms in each ward of his hospital with boards and put screens on their windows, thereby making them strong and indestructible. However, he did not oppose restraints in every case.

Dr. James L. Athon abandoned the muff and wristlet and only used the camisole on patients who removed their clothes. However, he did not like to use camisoles on suicidal patients because one of his patients had made a rope from one and used it to hang himself. Anthon used ether and chloroform with some benefit, either temporarily or permanently, on patients who had been in camisoles for months. With the violent insane, he used sulfate or manganese and tartarized antimony carried to the point of catharsis. That combination also gave an appetite to patients who refused to eat.

Dr. O.C. Kendrick placed camisoles and muffs on suicidal, impulsive, maniacal, or masturbating patients, and on others to prevent indecent exposure. Now and then, he isolated a patient with impulsive insanity for the safety of the other patients.[2]

Dr. Joseph A. Reed only used the muff and camisole, but rarely. Using depressing agents such as antimony and veratria (veratrum) as curatives was all right, but it was decidedly cruel to give medicine to repress a patient's violence in order to make his attendant's task easier. The evil resulting from such practices could be greater and more permanent than using the camisole.

Dr. T. R. H. Smith did not use fear to control his patients because he believed it was the lowest, most debasing and brutalizing of all motives. Instead, he appealed to the patient's pride and sentiments of religion, and praised him. He only used mild restraints for the shortest time possible on a patient who might injure himself, tear his clothes, or destroy everything within reach.

Smith confined a patient with a disposition to hurt others, in his room until his excitement wore off. However, protracted seclusion was more objectionable than mild restraints in the open air, or in cheerful, well-ventilated corridors. For the past twelve months, Smith frequently had used sulfuric ether with gratifying results to control such patients. Doing so often prevented paroxysm. In other cases, he used opiates, or some one of the anodynes with success. Sometimes a warm bath with cold applications to the head succeeded. He never used depressing remedies, alluded to by Dr. Athon, as doing so could be a hazardous practice. His hospital had a bedstrap, but he had never used it.[3]

When Dr. J. D. Barkdull took charge of his hospital two years earlier, he found ten to twelve patients, males and females, restrained by iron handcuffs, and several others restrained with camisoles. Many of them were kept in a picketed enclosure 20'x90' that was located in front of the buildings. Some patients had been in the enclosure for months, others for years. Barkdull subsequently learned that restraints had been used extensively since the hospital was established ten years earlier. Reasons given were lack of room for classification, crowded wards, and a lack of suitable accommodations for excited patients.

As soon as Barkdull satisfied himself that restraints had been abandoned or reduced elsewhere, he released those patients from the enclosure where they immediately enjoyed freedom, caused little trouble, and were less noisy. Bardull held his predecessor in high regard, and did not believe they should be held liable to charges of cruelty because summers in his part of the country were long with extreme heat.

Therefore, handcuffs were not as uncomfortable as a camisole that covered the upper part of the body would have been.

Dr. John P. Gray only used restraints for short periods when female patients removed their clothes or preceding and during menstruation. He also used the camisoles and bedstraps on those who suffered from acute mania, or on a patient who was inclined to get up at night and walk about. He believed that restraints had saved the lives of many of his patients who would otherwise have died from exhaustion.

Dr. R. Hills substituted personal attention for restraints, causing his attendants to often watch patients for hours to avoid using them. He confined a violent patient to his room, a darkroom, or a secure room until his violence abated. It usually lasted an hour or two; sometimes half a day; and on rare occasions, the entire day. By doing so, Hill reduced the total amount of reclusion without physical restraints.

When he had a suicidal patient who was not under personal surveillance, he placed him in a secure room with covered windows and transom gratings with fine wire gauze, and rounded off the corner of edges of woodwork. Therefore, a patient could not injure himself unless he butted his head against the wall. Hill believed that the patient was pretty safe, and could not dash his brains out in that manner.[4]

Dr. D. C. S. Choate used the camisole to prevent suicide and keep patients properly clothed. He strenuously objected to Dr. Hill's substitution of seclusion for mechanical restraint. In every case, seclusion in solitary rooms, was objectionable in the highest degree. Patients were certain to be neglected.

Instead of being kept out of sight, attendants should observe every change in the most difficult patients and only then carefully apply restraints. Choate observed that seclusion was the most frequent cause of deterioration in the habits of the insane. Patients acquired solitary vices and habits of destruction and filth, or if already learned, ones that most rapidly became fixed.

Choate used seclusion as a remedial agent, but not to replace restraints. With that view, seclusion could be free of abuse. Since the patience of attendants was not inexhaustible, there was a limit to their forbearance and benevolence. Therefore, he would rather trust such patients to the camisole instead of expecting the attendants to handle them.[5]

Dr. C. H. Nichols believed if restraints were necessary for the patient's welfare, it was important that they be applied in a gentle manner in the presence the superintendent or a responsible medical assistant. Exercise in the open air helped chronic cases, and it was better to have patients out-of-doors with restraints than to keep them inside in seclusion. They should not be kept in pens in close-walled yards like cattle caught astray. Instead, the caretakers should take them on daily, long walks, but not under public observation.

Nichols opposed using antimony, shower baths, the douche, and similar agents except for physical reasons. Caretakers should not try to reduce the patient's mental excitement by depressing their vital powers that could cause the cruel or even fatal, abuses. The superintendent or one of his assistants must be present and exert rigid supervision when caretakers were bathing timid and feeble male patients. An intelligent, female assistant should be provided when female patients were bathed. Carelessness often could do great harm to the patient by a bath that was too warm or too cold for his benefit, or if the attendant allowed him to remain too long, or if the bath was agreeable, not long enough.[6]

APPENDIX C

The Medical Treatment of Insanity as Described by Dr. Samuel B. Woodward

D r. Stribling did not summarize his medical treatments, however; they were probably very similar to those practiced by Dr. Samuel B. Woodward, M.D. of the Massachusetts State Lunatic Asylum. Stribling probably met Woodward in 1836 when he took a trip North to visit hospitals there for the insane. That the two doctors were friends is evidenced by the fact that Woodward visited Stribling in Staunton in 1844.

Woodward's peers showed their great respect for him when they elected him the first president "The Association of Medical Superintendents of American Institutions for the insane." His article entitled, "Observations on the Medical Treatment of Insanity" was read at the Superintendents' meeting inn May of 1846 and published in the *American Journal of Insanity, July, 1850.* Woodward's article follows.

"Moral influence is nearly as important in the treatment of any physical disease as in insanity. The mind must be managed, hope inspired, and confidence secured, to insure success in the treatment of any important disease.

All cases of insanity do not require a medical prescription. Many will recover spontaneously after a time, and many more by simple regulations of diet and such gentle means as will aid the powers of nature, in effecting salutary changes. This is also true of many other diseases affecting the vital organs. The judgment must be exercised in all cases to decide where to withhold and where to use remedies.

Insanity has been divided into mania, melancholia, and dementia, and each of these into acute and chronic forms. Whether or not these divisions embrace all of the forms of disease included under the general term, insanity, it is sufficient for the present purpose to give some account of these diseases with some of their complication, and the remedies that have been found useful in their treatment. In addition to those forms mentioned above, this paper will address Periodical Insanity; and Pulmonary.

Acute mania is the most violent and apparently the most formidable and dangerous form of insanity. Its accession is generally sudden, often violent, and its symptoms unequivocal. It is usually attended with increased heat of the head, frequent pulse, warm and soft skin, with extremities included to coldness, furred tongue, constipated bowels, sleeplessness, disposition to load talking, great volubility, disassociation of ideas, rapid changes of the feelings, impetuosity of manner, extravagance of expression, delusion, perversion of the moral, powers, disorder of the senses, and inordinate muscular strength. When at rest, the pulse is not often found to be hard or strong, neither is there much evidence of vascular excitement, but when the maniac puts forth his power in physical efforts, his strength is amazing, his power of endurance incredible, and an excitement is produced in the system which is a fallacious guide to the treatment.

Those who are not extensively acquainted with insanity frequently prescribe for this group of symptoms, as they would in phrenitis though the diseases vary essentially. In phrenitis the head is extremely painful, the arteries of the head and neck throb violently, the eyes are inflamed and light is intolerable. The pulse is hard and strong when the patient is at rest. The skin is hot and dry, the appetite gone, the strength prostrated, and the mind is affected with muttering delirium instead of maniacal excitement. Inflammation of the most acute character attends this disease. Not so with acute mania. The symptoms are different. The head is rarely painful, the eyes are not inflamed, light is seldom distressing, and sometimes there is great insensibility to it. The appetite is generally unimpaired, sometimes excessive, the pulse if full but not hard, the strength increased, not prostrated and the reaction, if there is any, not general, not affecting the extremities and the skin is in acute inflammation.

Mania

The medical treatment of mania may generally be commenced by a long continued warm bath, especially on going to bed and cold applications to the head, if agreeable to the patient. The bowels must be moved by a mercurial purge or other laxative. If it is then decided that opiates are appropriate remedies, the Dover's powder with small doses of calomel may be first used, and the solution of the sulfate of morphia, acetate of morphia, or the tincture of opium may be given either alone or with small does of Antimony, Ipecac, or Actoes Racemosa to determine to the surface.

The effect of these remedies should be carefully watched, and the dose increased or varied according to the effect. If the patient becomes more quiet the does may be gradually lessened, but the medicine should not be suddenly withdrawn lest the excitement return. If the excitement continues, the remedy may be increased gradually or rapidly till it controls the symptoms, produces quiet, and the mind becomes rational. The warm bath may be renewed if the effect is favorable, and cold may be applied to the head if there is much heat or if it is grateful to the patient. If the excitement is moderate, the case may be left for a time without medicine, or the milder narcotics may be tried. If however, narcotics are indicated, no substitute can be found for these different preparations of opium. The strengths must be supported by good nourishment, diffusible stimulants, and tonics if needed, and all the appliances moral and physical that can be useful should be added to the medical treatment to insure a favorable restoration to health.

Acute Mania

The treatment of acute mania differs considerably from that mania. Depletion, as such, either local or general, will rarely be indicated. The period of vascular excitement, if it has ever existed, is past. When the patient is quiet, the head is not hot, neither is the pulse excited not accelerated. If there is any increased heat about the head, the extremities will be cold, and the motion of the capillary vessels deficient. The functions of digestion are often well performed, the appetite is good, sometimes excessive. In many cases there is no apparent derangement of the physical system which indicate medical treatment except the insanity itself.

If the health is not good, the first object should be to improve it. The condition of all the important organs of the body should be attentively examined before the case is abandoned as hopeless. The appetite, apparently good, may be morbid, the functions of the liver may be disturbed, the bowels may be constipated, the evacuations may be unhealthy or a tendency to diarrhea may exist. The functions of the skin are often badly performed, the secretion is deficient or unhealthy, and a peculiar fetor attends it. The functions of the uterus are frequently disturbed, and an unnatural irritation in that organ affects the general health and gives character to the symptoms of mental alienation.

The warm and cold baths, laxatives, alternatives, deobstruents, tonics, narcotics, a generous diet and active exercise are often indicated in different forms and stages of chronic mania. If the liver is diseased or inactive, the bile vitiated or deficient, and the bowels torpid, mercurials will be indicated for a time, and tonics and narcotics accompany or follow their use. The Conium with iron is a useful combination to effect salutary changes in the secretions of the liver, to quiet the irritability and restlessness of the patients, and promote sleep. The does must be large to produce any perceptible effect. In some cases, other preparations of iron combined with narcotics and diffusible stimulants, answer the purpose equally well.

Malt liquors, porter, ale, and strong beer are much used in some foreign institutions, and may be prescribed with advantage in many cases. Porter and limewater in equal quantities, form one of the best remedies to invigorate the system, to correct the stomach when dyspeptic, and promote sleep.

In chronic mania, there is rarely continued excitement; some periodicity is apparent and in the intervals, neuralgia is frequently troublesome, affecting the face, teeth, and limbs, causing much suffering, and greatly increasing the irritability of the patient. When the excitement comes on, all these symptoms vanish, and a violent mania, equal in severity to a recent attack, continues for some days. In proportion to the length and severity of this excitement will be the corresponding depression and melancholy, and the case will continue in this way for many years.

In this form of insanity the mind is less liable to become demented than when either melancholy or mania continues with little or no interruption, and the case is more hopeful of cure than most others found, of chronic mania. Whatever tends to lessen the excitement in one condition, or prevent or remove the melancholy in the other, will diminish the severity of the disease, and aid in accomplishing the cure. Most such cases are but little affected by medicine; some however, yield favorably to its influence, and finally recover. The diet and regimen that will produce the most perfect bodily health, with tonics, stimulates, and narcotics have a favorable tendency in this form of mania. In no case is the perseverance in the use of means attended by more encouraging results.

In some cases, full does of opium are very effective in diminishing the violence of the excitement and preventing the severity of the following depression. A consequence of this remedy for a long period has finally resulted in the removal of the disease, and a complete restoration to health.

Such favorable results cannot be anticipated in a majority of the cases.

The long continued use of Conium and Iron in large doses, occasionally effects favorably changes, and is worth a fair trial; especially if neuralgia intervenes between the paroxysms of excitement. This remedy is not at all calculated for acute mania, certainly not till the active symptoms have subsided, but in chronic mania its use is often indicated. These indications are torpor of the liver, neuralgia, unhealthy secretions of the intestinal and dermoid surfaces, amenorrhoes, dysmenorrhoes, glandular enlargements, general strumous habit, dyspepsia with gastrodynia and an irritable excited state of the nervous system often observable in insanity, producing irascibility, restlessness, indescribable peevishness, discontent, and variableness of feeling.

Sometimes this remedy will relieve the symptoms before its narcotic effect is distinctly perceived, sometimes slight narcosis takes place before relief is procured, but in general, its full effect is not felt in relieving the disease for which it is prescribed till narcosis, more or less obvious, is produced. These effects are slight vertigo, pain over the eyes, gastric sinking and faintness and coldness of the extremities. It is safe to give the medicine in gradually increasing doses till these results are produced, and it may be continued with entire safety for months, the doses being occasionally increased to show that the nervous system is under its influence.

Nitrate of Silver in combination with narcotics, is often a valuable remedy in mania where there is an epileptic tendency, or where the actions of the heart are involved in disease. Sulfate of Zinc, Quinine, the arsenical solution, Nux Vomica, Guaiacum, aromatics, and all the list of diffusible stimulants are useful to fulfill certain indications and promote the general health.

If the mind has not become demented, no case if chronic mania should be abandoned till all appliances, medical and moral, that the case may indicate, have had a fair trial, and even failure under some circumstances should not discourage further attempts to make impressions upon a disease, the symptoms of which sometimes recur only in obedience to established habits, and not from any organic lesion of the brain.

Acute or Recent Melancholy

The attack of melancholy is general less sudden than that of mania; the symptoms come on gradually and progress slowly; the health is more generally and obviously impaired. In melancholy, one subject, and frequently, a single idea, occupies the mind. It may be property, reputation, the present or future well being of the person afflicted, that engrosses the thoughts and overwhelms the mind with agitation and alarm. With the melancholic there is no present enjoyment, no hope, no confidence, every thing wears a gloomy aspect, every contemplation is sad, and nature, with all its loveliness, is somber, darkened and cheerless.

In cases of this description, the health usually suffers sometime before the mind exhibits impairment. The digestive organs are often involved in disease, the biliary secretions are deficient or unhealthy, the bowels are torpid, the evacuations dark, glutinous, and offensive, the appetite is often deficient or morbid, the tongue is furred, though sometimes clean, smooth and often red, the skin is unusually dry, frequently cold, and the capillary action sluggish.

In the treatment of melancholy, the first object is to remove the obvious symptom of the disease and improve the general health. The bowels should be cleaned by calomel or blue pill, which may be occasionally repeated, care being taken that salivation be avoided, as this effect of mercury is not desirable. After the first improvement is made upon the secretions by mercurial remedies, other laxatives may be substituted which will keep the bowels regularly open, and least disturb the stomach or reduce the strength. Drastic purges are rarely if ever indicated, but sometimes active remedies are required to produce moderate effects when the bowels are quite torpid.

It was in this form of insanity that the ancients prescribed hellebore successfully, and considered it little less than a specific. This medicine is nauseating and drastic, and finds little favor in modern practice.

The infusion of Senna, pills of Aloes, and Colocynth, extract of Butternut, and especially the Guaiacum in tincture or powder, answer well to obviate constipation. The Guaiacum possesses other medical qualities besides its powers as a laxative. It is a favorable stimulant, improving the appetite, invigorating the muscular fiber of the bowels, promoting the action of the capillary vessels of the skin, and, in amenorrhoes, acting favorably on the uterus. It may be given in doses much larger than usually prescribed if necessary to obtain its laxative effects. After it has been used for some time, constipation does not frequently follow when it is omitted; it leaves a positive effect in habits of constipation.

Next in value to those remedies that make favorable impressions upon the digestive organs, are those that act upon the skin. Baths, friction, and counter irritants are often useful.

When the skin is dry, and the capillary action sluggish, warm and tepid baths followed by friction, are valuable remedies. The invigorating effects of the cold bath and shower bath, followed by friction, are often useful in this form of insanity. This will hardly fail to be true if reaction speedily follows their use. If, however, chilliness, coldness and paleness of the surface follow, and little or no reactions takes place after them, the warm or tepid bath will be found to do better. In many cases, pediluvium answers a better purpose than general bathing, especially if extremities are inclined to be cold, and the blood is too much determined in the head. Medicated footbaths are often valuable remedies. For this purpose, mustard, common salt, or the nitro-muriatic acid may be used with benefit.

In many cases of insanity, blisters are of doubtful utility, they often produce, rather than allay, irritation, and promote, rather than control excitement; but in some cases of melancholy, especially if there is disease of the digestive organs, and tenderness of the epigastric region, blisters applied over the part are valuable remedies. The tincture of Iodine applied externally, instead of blisters, often answers a valuable purpose and produces less irritation. The antimonial ointment has also the same good effect, but is often more painful than blisters, and sometimes disturbs the stomach with nausea and vomiting.

Tonics and stimulants are valuable remedies in melancholy. Quinine, Iron bitters, aromatics, malt liquors, and other diffusible stimulants, answer a good purpose, in many cases, either alone or in combination with laxatives. The milder narcotics are often useful in allying irritation and promoting sleep. Conium, Hyoscyamus, Camphor, and

Lupuline, may be described for this purpose with advantage, but in many cases the preparations of opium are better than all medicines for this object. Opium does not usually require to be given in such full doses in melancholy as in mania, and night doses do better in the former than in the latter disease.

The combination of Conium and Iron is better adapted to melancholy than mania; its deobstruent effects are often as necessary as its tonic influence, and the combination is a more efficient remedy than either of the articles alone. In neuralgia, attending melancholy, its effects are often very beneficial, also in cases attended by glandular enlargements, indicating scrofula.

The combination of the extract of Hyoscyamus, Campthorm and Lapuline often promotes sleep when other remedies fail, but where decided narcotic influence is required the preparations of opium are decidedly the best, and are more to be relied upon than all others. In certain cases of melancholy the patients made tranquil and comparatively happy by the use of this remedy, the sleep becomes more quiet, and under its influence the person is able to pursue labor and amusement, when without it his suffering and despondency would wholly prevent him from engaging in any employment. Opiates are particularly indicated in suicidal cases by relieving the extreme suffering which impels to that fatal and deplorable act.

Setons, issues and cupping may be beneficial in certain cases of melancholy, especially where there have been eruptions, permanent or repelled, and where habitual ulcers have ceased to discharge. In ordinary cases they avail little in improving the condition of the patient, but, by the irritation which they excited, sometimes do injury.

Riding and other exercise, amusements, labor, whatever diverts the mind or improves the health of the patient, is of importance in the treatment of melancholy. Confidence in the medical adviser, and encouragement constantly held forth to the sufferer, greatly aid the effect of remedies. Perseverance with medicine often achieves good when a short trial is attended with little or no benefit.

Chronic, or Long Continued Melancholy

In all cases of insanity which have passed into a chronic state, where the health is not good and medical treatment has been neglected, a trial of remedies should be made. If the disease is not cured, the condition of the patient may be improved, the health made better, the sufferings diminished, and the enjoyments increased. The symptoms should be examined with care and every circumstance of health attended to. Constipation, habitual and obstinate often attends chronic melancholy, morbid appetite is also common, and the functions of the liver are performed imperfectly, or in an unhealthy manner. The state of the skin is frequently bad, and cleanliness has generally been neglected.

To remedy this, baths are indispensable. Exercise, a very important means of cure, is usually but little attended to, and the extremities become cold, peculiarly soft and livid. With these evidences of physical derangement the mind dwells intently on one subject, broods over it to the neglect of every other till its sphere of action becomes extremely limited. Under these circumstances he energies of physical power, no less than those of the mind, become greatly prostrated, general debility and listlessness follow, exertion is painful and difficult, and no ordinary effort of the individual can relieve this condition of apathy and prostration.

All the appliances of art should be held in requisition to arouse the dormant physical and mental energies. Tonics, alternatives, baths, frictions, purgatives, external and internal stimulants, generous diet, exercise, and narcotics may, in different cases, or in succession in the same case, be found useful. Occasionally one individual may be cured, many may be made essentially better, while with some, all remedies will fail, and the patient, by imperceptible changes, will grow worse, and finally become permanently demented.

Chronic and Acute Dementia

Dementia is a term usually applied to a state of disease in which the mind is so weakened as to afford little or no hope of improvement. It commonly follows long continued mania and melancholy, and in most cases, is probably the effect of organic disease of the brain. The disease, of course, is rarely cured, and can hardly be said to be a subject for medical treatment, except so far as the general health is impaired. In many such cases the health is bad, and the habits of life are perverted. Both medical and moral treatment may here be beneficial. There is often derangement of the digestive organs, vitiated appetite, constipation of the bowels, and a bad condition of the skin, which may be remedied. Baths, laxatives, tonics, and perseverance in the efforts to correct impaired and irregular habits, will greatly improve the condition of the patient. In such cases the brain is not always irreparably injured; great debility and extreme inaction produces the phenomena instead of organic lesion.

Acute Dementia

There is a form of dementia of recent accession in which the symptoms assume the character of this disease quite early after the attack, which is hopeful, and in which medical treatment is very successful. The appearance of the patient does not differ essentially from the protracted and chronic form. The physiognomy of the case may not be quite so bad, but the indications of loss of mind are nearly as distinct. The length of time which the symptoms have existed being less, the encouragement for the trial of remedies is greater, and the success of them is often exceedingly favorable. The treatment is various, according to the symptoms of the case. Alternative and laxative remedies, baths, tonics, aromatics, stimulants, blisters and irritants are indicated in various forms and stages of the disease. Exercise, active and passive, friction and every means of arousing the mind from its torpor and invigorating the system, will be found useful auxiliaries in the treatment of this form of insanity.

Periodical Insanity

No form of insanity is more troublesome to manage, or as difficult to cure, than this, especially if it assumes at periods the two extremes of violent mania, and deep melancholy.

Both cases have, at each occasion, all the symptoms of recent mania, and at their period of depression the discouragement, wretchedness, and suicidal tendency of the most marked recent melancholy. These transitions take place at different periods, sometimes annually, semi-annually, and at shorter intervals. The violence of one form of the disease may generally be predicted by the severity of the other. The condition of the mind in the transition state differs considerably, and this is longer or shorter in different cases. In some cases the mind seems to be nearly rational for a long period; in others, the delusions remain though the excitement subsides, and the extremes of the case are at long intervals. Sometimes the transition is very sudden, and the patient is most of the time greatly excited or much depressed. Some cases recover after years of suffering, in others the paroxysms diminish in frequency and intensity, and the patient is greatly improved if not entirely cured.

The treatment of this form of insanity may be conducted upon the principles before mentioned as applicable to the acute forms of mania and melancholy, with the use of such remedies in the interval as will tend to break up the periodicity of the disease. If, by the use of remedies, the excitement can be lessened, the corresponding depression will probably be less; so if extreme melancholy can be prevented the succeeding excitement will be less severe.

In such cases it is of the greatest importance that all the causes which have a tendency to bring on the renewed attack of disease be cautiously avoided. The health should be preserved as perfect as possible, all excitement should be shunned, especially that intensity of application of mind or body that tends to disturb the nervous system and bring it within the range of the disease. By these means confirmed habits of periodicity may, doubtless, be avoided, in many cases, and the recovery may be perfect. If the business or occupation of a person affected with insanity is suspected to act as a cause of disease, it should be abandoned, and such others chosen as will have no such tendency, but rather a counteracting influence.

The sedentary should become active, the irregular should become systematic, and those who are fond of excitements should avoid them. In this manner many may escape a return of disease and periodicity be avoided. There are many discouragements in these cases but hope may be entertained while the mind retains its vigor and the physical energies continue. The best efforts will, however, sometimes prove abortive, and though remedies may be used, the disease will remain unchanged, and a long life be spent in the extreme of this form of insanity.

When the maniacal excitement subsides in periodical insanity, neuralgia of the limbs, joints, teeth or face, often follows, and severe bodily suffering attends he gloom and wretchedness of the mental depression. In this form of disease the health is nor usually good, this is more manifest in the period of depression. The remedies usually prescribed in neuralgia succeed in relieving the suffering of the patient, and improve the health. Of these preparations of opium, bark, Nux Vomica, Conium and Iron, the arsenical solution, and Veratrine, are the most effectual.

Puerperal Insanity

Insanity occurring in the puerperal state is a dangerous complication, and requires some modification of the treatment usually pursued. The symptoms are generally severe, the mania furious, and the indications of physical disease considerable. The hot skin, frequent pulse, wild delirium, and coated tongue resemble inflammation so strongly that there is a danger of mistaking the case, and adopting a course of treatment which these deceptive symptoms seem to indicate. General bleeding is rarely useful, but leeching may often afford present relief and prepare the system for other remedies. Cold applications to the head give much relief, and local warm bathing to the feet, at the same time, or a general warm bath may be frequently beneficial. Calomel alone or in combination with Dover's powder may then be given till it moves the bowels freely, and be repeated in small doses till the secretions are favorably affected, the skin becomes soft, and the tongue moist. If the insanity continues, the preparation of morphia may then be given in such doses as the patients will bear, cautiously watching its effects. If they are favorable, the symptoms usually subside rapidly, the case terminates favorably, and the recovery is soon complete. Tonics and stimulants often aid in the speedy restoration to health.

Insanity Complicated by Dyspepsia

Dyspepsis is frequently found to be the cause of insanity, and is often complicated with it when not strictly the cause. Obstinate constipation attends many cases, and such a total loss of appetite and loathing of food that the patient will often suffer from starvation if not urged and persuaded to take nourishment. Patients frequently vomit their food and have great derangement of the secretions of the stomach, flatulency acidity, and morbid bile. Diarrhea with red and dry tongue is worse than constipation, and is an unfavorable complication of the disease. Constipation is easily obviated and produces less ill effect than would be supposed, buy diarrhea is often difficult to control, and when it has been suppressed it will recur again from the slightest cause.

Tonics, laxatives, baths, gentle exercise, friction, and a proper regulation of diet, constitute the treatment of insanity with this combination of symptoms. Astringents, aromatics, and moderate opiates are indicated when diarrhea is present. If acidity is troublesome, attended with loss of appetite, one of the best remedies is a combination of lime water with porter or strong beer. If with constipation there is distress from food, the aromatic tincture of guaiacum is little less than a specific, when given in doses sufficiently large to prove laxative. In recent cases of dysentery and diarrhea, emetics of Ipecac and sulfate of zinc often prove useful, followed by opiates, nitrate of silver, Capsicum and other aromatics. In chronic cases, in addition to those remedies, the tincture of Zanthorrhiza is found very useful given in brandy and water or milk. Severe dyspepsia complicated with insanity often results in fatal maramus, of which diarrhea is usually one of the most troublesome symptoms. This disease if probably the most frequent fatal termination of insanity.

Pulmonary Consumption

This is second on the list of fatal diseases with the insane, showing that the character of the brain is often scrofulous in its origin. In some cases disease of the lungs and of the brain alternate. When the excitement is great, the cough and expectoration abate or cease; when the excitement subsides the cough returns and the expectoration is abundant. The occurrence of insanity occasionally suspends the symptoms of pulmonary disease, but they recur and prove fatal when insanity is cured.

A rapid consumption is frequently the fatal event of insanity. The form of dyspeptic Phthisis is also frequent with the insane. This disease requires no peculiarity of treatment.

Erysipelas is a troublesome disease with the insane and often assumes a dangerous and fatal form. Erysipelas of the extremities is much more to be dreaded than that of the face. When it is suppurative it is rapid and requires very prompt treatment.

The application of strong tincture of Iodine to the inflamed surface and beyond the margin, on the very commencement of the disease, is an exceedingly successful remedy. Should the disease pass the line made by the application of the Iodine, it may be extended farther, till it shall arrest the progress of the inflammation and convert a disease which might have been dangerous and fatal, into a comparatively mild and harmless affection. A circle made beyond the boundary of the disease, by the nitrate of silver or of the Lytta, often answers the same valuable purpose. Another useful practice is, to puncture the inflamed limb repeatedly with numerous incisions, thus allowing the infiltrated pus to escape, and removing the distention which greatly aggravates the suffering of the patient. The constitutional remedies in this form of disease are, first alteratives and laxatives, followed by tonics, stimulants, narcotics, and good liquid

Disease of the heart, of the uterus, and neuralgia, often attend insanity but require no peculiar treatment.

Amenorrhea is frequently considered a cause of insanity, and its removal is looked to as a sure indication of cure. In this there is often disappointment. Whatever indicates returning health is favorable in insanity. When the health improves, in recent cases, before there is any particular change in the state of mind, the indication is favorable. So far the return of the menses gives encouragement. They are restored in many cases, however, without any obvious change in the symptoms. The menstrual period is often attended by increased excitement, and this is quite as likely to follow as to precede or accompany discharge. In such cases the suspension of the menses is attended by favorable results till the general health is improved and the irritable state of the uterus, and general health is improved, and the irritable state of the uterus, and general nervous system is allayed or removed. In cases where the periods of excitement are connected with the menstrual visitation, the occurrence of pregnancy and the final cessation of the menses has been attended by favorable results, even by a radical cure.

Mecurial and aloetic purges, tincture of Guiaiasum, the various preparations of iron with or without Conium, are to be relied upon in amenorrhea, but they effect a cure by improving the general health rather than by any specific effect upon the uterus itself.

It has been remarked that the insane are peculiarly liable to neuralgia, especially when the disease is paroxysmal.

It is most successfully treated by narcotics and tonics. Morphia, Conium, Nux Vomica, Belladouna, arsenical solution, Quinine, Iron, Zinc, and Nitrate of Silver, are all valuable remedies, and should be used if necessary, administered freely. Belladouna, Veratrine, and cold water applied externally, often relieve the pain remarkably.

There are cases of insanity in which there is at first, high excitement, but in a few days there is an alarming collapse with symptoms of great exhaustion and debility. The head and chest are unusually hot, while the extremities are cold, purple, and covered with perspiration. The actions of the heart are feeble, often irregular. The pulse is exceedingly weak, and, in fatal case, ceases at the wrist long before the brain dies. These cases indicate danger from the first, and must be treated promptly or fatal symptoms will occur unexpectedly.

The bowels should be gently moved by calomel, and small doses of this remedy may be continued for a few days. Cold should be applied to the head, and blisters, sinapisms and rubefacients to the extremities and the chest. Great care should be taken not to exhaust the strength, and the vital powers should be sustained by a free use of volatile and diffusible stimulants, and good liquid nourishment. If opium is given, it should be in small doses combined with calomel, and at short intervals. Large doses fail to quiet the excitement, and in some cases seem to coincide with other influences to increase the delirium and irritation of the brain.

The views of experienced men at the present day, as to the treatment of insanity, differ greatly from those that were usually promulgated at the commencement of the present century. If there is a difference of opinion as to the necessity of treatment in various cases of insanity, there is great unanimity of sentiment in this country and in Great Britain, as to the indications of cure and the kind of remedies most to be relied upon when they are to be used.

The abandonment of depletion, external irritants, drastic purges and starvation, and the substitution of baths, narcotics, tonics, and generous diet, is not less to be appreciated in the improved condition of the insane, than the change from manacles, chains, by-locks and confining chairs, to the present system of kindness, confidence, social intercourse, labor, religious teaching and freedom from restraint. In this age of improvement, no class of mankind have felt its influence more favorably than the insane.

But we should not be satisfied with present attainments. Much undoubtedly remains to be done for them. Good influences are everywhere operating, and we may confidently hope that what is overlooked by the passing generation, which might have been beneficial to them, will be supplied by their successors."

APPENDIX D

Western State Statistics–1825-1871

I n Stribling's annual report to his directors for the years 1869-1871, he briefly described Western State as it then exited. Then he provided details on how it evolved. Stribling wrote:

> This is a brief statement as to the origin of an institution, which now affords comfortable accommodations for 350 patients. The buildings are of brick, neat in style and substantial in construction, covered with tin, warmed by steam, lighted with gas, and amply supplied with pure water, from a source so elevated as that forcing apparatus is unnecessary to distribute it about the grounds, or conduct it over the buildings.
>
> There are attached about 190 acres of land, not in all respects suitable for the demands of such an institution, but affording means of occupation to many of the inmates. And aiding materially, both as regards economy and comfort, in promoting the objects for which the hospital was founded.
>
> For many of the details of interest bearing upon the history of the institution, from the date of its establishment to the present time, you are respectfully referred to the following tables. These have been

prepared with care and the contents obtained from records now on file. Your attention is particularly asked to the synopsis, headed, "Recapitulation," showing the aggregate cost of land, buildings, covered ways, enclosures, water, steam and gas works. It will be found to compare most favorable with any similar institution in the United States.

Recapitulations of tables 1 through 9 follow.

Land	$8,505
Buildings	135,177
Covered Ways	5,665
Enclosures	20,842
Water Works	19,743
Steam Works	21,370
Gas Works	5,000
Total	$216,302

Table 1: Physician, Physician & Superintendent, Assistant Physician, Keeper, Stewards

Physician, Physician & Superintendents

William Boys,	May 26, 1828	June 30, 1836
F.T. Stribling,	July 1, 1836	July 1, 1840

Assistant Physicians:

Richard H. Gambill	Aug. 20, 1842	Dec. 31, 1857
Edward Fisher	Jan. 1, 1850	June 30, 1861
William Hamilton	July 1, 1851	present time
T. Van L. Davis	July 1, 1858	Dec. 31, 1864
Richard H. Gambill	Jan. 1, 1865	Dec. 19, 1865
Thomas A. Berkley	Jan. 5, 1866	present time

Keeper:

Samuel M. Woodward	Aug. 27, 1827	July 1, 1840

Stewards:

Samuel M. Woodward	July 1, 1840	Dec. 31, 1862
Samuel Hoshour	Jan. 1, 1863	present time

Table 2: Land

Year	Cost (in dollars)
1825	600
1828	300
1838	2,325
1839	1,000
1840	785
1846	968
1847	301
1848	226
Total	$8505

Table 3: Buildings

1825-28	21,100
1833	6,000
1834	9,000
1835	1,500
1836	6,000
1838	12,000
1841	340
1842	16,685
1843	8,194
1844	7,984
1846	197
1848	6,982
1849	19,642
1850	9,376
1851	537

1860	4,547
1861	5,093
Total	$135,177

Table 4 Covered Ways:

1857	719
1857	4,945
Total	$5,665

Table 5: Enclosures, Iron, Brick and Wood

1830	5,000
1835	1,500
1855	6,733
1857	3,397
1858	233
1859	353
1860	178
1861	178
1862	3,041
1863	231
Total	$20,842

Table 6: Water Works

1833	$1,000
1835	1,200
1839	5,000

1842	2,000
1857	1,869
1858	435
1859	8,060
1861	178
Total	$19,743

Table 7: Steam Works:

1854	8,407
1855	8,020
1856	272
1857	878
1858	3,794
Total	$21,370

Table 8: Gas Works:

1852	$4,241
1853	759
Total	$5,000

Table 9: Average number of patients

1828	15
1829-30	30
1831	35
1832-35	36
1836	48

1837	63	1851	293
1838	69	1852	326
1839	72	1853	359
1840	70	1854-55	382
1841	84	1856-57	389
1842	104	1858-59	381
1843	114	1860-61	376
1844	131	1862-63	356
1845	163	1864-65	319
1846	200	1865-66	323
1847(9 months)	208	1867	323
1848	206	1868-69	331(1)
1849	210	1870-71	—
1850	246		

APPENDIX E

Insanity in the United States in 1840

(Based on the 1840 Census)

S tribling gave the following information in his introduction to the Table 1 that follows:

> From the census of 1840 I have been enabled to select the following interesting statistics in relation to insanity as it exists in North America.
>
> The annexed table will exhibit the number of insane and idiotic whites,
>
> Free colored and slaves in each of the state and territories, and is so arrange to show—first, the number of white lunatics and idiots, both at public and private charge, and the proportion of these to the population in each state.
>
> Second, the number of free blacks who are insane or idiotic in each state, and the proportion which they bear to its free colored population. And third, the number of slaves, insane or idiotic, and proportion of these to the slave population of the respective states, with a summary, exhibiting the total of each of these classes, and their proportion to the aggregate population of the Union.

Note: Table 1 has been divided into two parts: the first whites and second, free colored and blacks in order to make it more legible.

Table 1 - Statistics on the White Insane

	Public Expense	Private Expense	Total	Population	% to Population
ME	207	330	537	500438	1 to 932
NH	180	306	486	284036	1 to 584
MA	471	600	1071	720030	1 to 680
RI	117	86	203	105587	1 to 520
CT	114	384	498	301856	1 to 606
VT	144	254	398	291218	to 731
NY	683	1463	2146	2378890	1 to 1108
NJ	144	225	369	351588	1 to 952
PA	469	1477	1946	1676115	1 to 861
DE	22	30	52	58561	1 to 1126
MD	133	254	387	317717	1 to 821
VA	317	731	1048	740968	1 to 707
NC	152	428	680	484870	1 to 836
SC	91	285	376	259084	1 to 689
GA	51	243	294	407695	1to1386
AL	31	193	232	335185	1 to 1444
MS	14	102	116	179074	1 to 1543
LA	6	49	55	158457	1 to 2880
TN	103	596	699	640627	1 to 916
KY	305	490	795	590253	1 to 742
OH	363	832	1195	1502122	1 to 1257
IN	110	377	487	678698	1 to 1393
Il	36	177	213	472254	1 to 2217
MO	42	160	202	32388	1 to 1603
AR	9	36	45	77174	1 to 1715
MI	2	37	39	211560	1 to 5294
FL	1	9	10	27943	1 to 2704
WI	1	7	8	30749	1 to 3843
IA	2	5	7	42924	1 to 6132
DC	1	13	14	30657	1 to 2189

Totals for Whites

	Insane	Population	Proportion of Insane
Whites	14,508	14,189,218	1 to 978

Table 2 - Free Blacks and Slaves

	Insane Black	Total Blacks	Propr. Blacks	Insane Slaves	Total Slaves	Propr. Insane
ME	94	1355	1 to 14			
NH	19	537	1 to 28	-		1
MA	200	8668	1 to 43			
RI	13	3238	1 to 249	5		
CT	44	8105	1 to 184	17		
VT	13	730	1 to 56			
NY	194	50027	1 to 257	4		
NJ	73	21044	1 to 288	674		
PA	187	47854	1 to 255	64		
DE	7	16919	1 to 2417	21	2605	1 to 124
MD	42	62020	1 to 1476	99	89495	1 to 904
VA	58	49842	1 to 859	326	448987	1 to 1377
NC	29	22732	1 to 783	192	245817	1 to 1280
SC	16	8276	1 to 517	121	327038	1 to 2702
GA	26	2753	1 to 106	108	280944	1 to 2601
AL	25	2039	1 to 81	100	253532	1 to 2635
MI	16	1369	1 to 85	66	195211	1 to 2957
LA	7	25502	1 to 3643	38	168452	1 to 4432
TN	28	5524	1 to 197	124	183059	1 to 1476
KY	48	7317	1 to 152	132	182258	1 to 1380
OH	165	17342	1 to 105	-	3	
ID	75	7165	1 to 95	-	3	
IL	79	3598	1 to 45	-	331	
MO	18	1574	1 to 87	50	58240	1 to 1164
AR	8	465	1 to 58	13	19935	1 to 1534
MI	26	707	1 to 27			
FL	-	817	-	12	25517	1 to 2143
WI	3	185	1 to 61	-	11	
IO	4	172	1 to 43	16		
DC	3	8361	1 to 2767	4	4694	1 to 1173

Totals of Free Blacks and Slaves

	Insane	Population	Proportion of Insane
Free blacks	1,520	386, 237	1 to 254
Slaves	1,406	2,487,112	1 to 1769

Totals: Whites, Free Blacks and Slaves

	Insane	Population	Proportion of Insane
Whites	1450	14,189, 218	1 to 978
Free Blacks	1520	386, 237	1 to 254
Slaves	1,406	2,487,112	1 to 1769
Aggregate	17,434	17,062,567	1 to 978

Excerpts from comments made by Dr. Stribling follow that show Stribing's compassion for the plight of Virginia's insane.

> Where were the one thousand and more poor creatures, who have been deprived? of the God-like attribute of reason? And what is their present condition? We know, that but about two hundred and fifty of them are in the asylums of the Commonwealth, and are of course left to conjectures, as to the location and circumstances of the remainder. Many are doubtless with their friends, receiving all the attention which affection can bestow, and surrounded by every comfort which in their unhappy state they can appreciate, but their disease is doubtless becoming more firmly riveted by every day's duration, and many of them it may be, already doomed to continue its victims during life. Others are wretched wanderers, traversing the highways or by-paths of the Commonwealth, unprotected and uncared for, suffering with cold and hunger, and exhibiting wherever they go, an exterior, but too well harmonizing with a "mind in ruins."

Whilst a third and most hapless class, are immured in the gloomy prisons of the country, degraded to a level with the criminal who has violated the laws both of God and man; chained like wild beasts to the floors of their grated cells; but half fed and altogether naked; often writhing too under the lash of their cruel keeper, and in this state, are cut off from intercourse with all living creatures, save, indeed, the creeping vermin which feed upon the filth in which their bodies are incased. Would that this picture were the result of fancy, or was even a reality somewhat exaggerated; but alas! For the honor of Virginia, it is too faithful a representation of what many of this class of unfortunates are now suffering with her borders; and whilst no one could be more unwilling than myself to do aught by which her fair fame might be tarnished, it would surely seem in this particular a false delicacy to disguise the truth, if its disclosures could by possibility lead to the rescue of a single one of these unhappy sufferers."

Then Stribling commented on the black insane.

It would seem from this exhibition, that the *free blacks* are much oftener the victims of this malady than either of the other classes, there being nearly four times as many of them in proportion as of the whites, and seven times as many of the slaves. The fact will also appear, from the examination of the foregoing table, that free colored persons residing in non-slaveholding states are much oftener the subjects of insanity than the same class who reside in the slave states, being in the former as *one* to *every one-hundred and forty-three*, whilst in the latter they are only as *one* to each *six hundred and fifty* of the free colored population.

Should not this disclosure have the effect to remind our *good abolition friends* at the North, of a Christian proverb, which it would seem (from having proffered their charity to those residing at so remote a distance from them) must have escaped their recollection? Surely, if this picture is true, the *poor blacks* at home, must be in a state of destitution both physical and moral, such as to afford ample scope for the exercise of their sympathy and benevolence, unit at least these should be solicited from a proper source in behalf of southern interests and southern institutions.(1)

Stribling seemed defensive when he commented on the differences between the numbers of insane blacks in the slaveholding states in the South with those of the non-holding ones in the North. His remarks confirm his pro-slavery views that were held by southerners at that time. Stribling further emphasized his views by placing some of the information in italics.

Stribling probably was not happy when Dr. Edward Jarvis immediately challenged the information in the 1840 Census and worked to have the report revised.

Additional Images

The following figures did not fit as well within the text as others did, but they are presented here because they are pertinent to Dr. Stribling's story.

IMAGE 36

Night Watchman's Clock.
(Courtesy, Western State Hospital)

IMAGE 37

Mail Pouch.
(Courtesy of Western State Hospital)

IMAGE 38

Cooking Pot.
(Courtesy, Western State Hospital.)

IMAGE 39

Coffee Grinder.
(Courtesy, Western State Hospital.)

IMAGE 40

Coffee Pot
(Courtesy, Western State Hospital.)

IMAGE 41

Seam sealer for tin roofs.
(Courtesy, Western State Hospital.)

IMAGE 42

Seed Separator.
(Courtesy, Western State Hospital.)

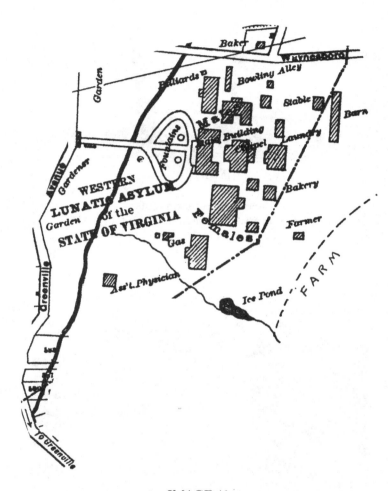

IMAGE 43

1884 Map, buildings that probably existed
during Stribling's Tenure.
(From *Annals of Augusta County by
Joseph Waddell, 1885.*)

IMAGE 44

Contemporary picture of Western State Hospital.
(Courtesy of Western State Hospital.)

IMAGE 45

Contemporary View of Western State hospital's Cementery.
(Courtesy of Western State Hospital)

ACKNOWLEDGEMENTS

D r. Brooks Barnes, librarian at Eastern Shore Library, read numerous drafts of the Stribling manuscript. Without his patience and guidance, I would have been unable to tell Stribling's story. Good friends Cap Mattie and Edward Menaker, decd., supported me in a variety of endeavors over many years.

At Western State Hospital, John Beghtol, Rick Will, Peter Grimm, and many others encouraged and guided me. Marty S. Kline at Eastern State hospital did the same. Tommy Rosen, long dedicated to saving Western State's artifacts, shared information on the antique clocks at Western State.

The following people took time from their own work to carefully read and comment on my manuscript: Dr. Kenneth Keller, head of the history department at Mary Baldwin College; Nancy Sorrels, supporter of the Augusta County Historical Society for years, and Gina Snell, Waynesboro civic leader and former mental health advocate in the area. Also J. Rankin of Dry Bone Press, and last, but not least, Mr. Ivan Dee, of Ivan Dee Publisher who was kind enough to read my manuscript and comment on it.

The following people have helped me in a variety of ways over the years, often guiding me to information that I had not known existed: John B. Davis and his staff at the Augusta County Courthouse; Karen Vest and Dot Reinbold at the Waynesboro Library; Michael Plunkett and his staff at Special Collections, University of Virginia Library; Leslie Morris at Houghton Library, Harvard University; various staff members of the Library of Virginia; Catherine Grosfils, formerly at the Colonial Williamsburg Foundation; and Professor Thomas Brown at the University of South Carolina. Over the years, I also have frequently turned to Col. Robert Driver for information on Confederate units and soldiers.

Special thanks to Kerford Brooks who, in spite of crowded objects and poor lighting, created many photographs of artifacts at Western State Hospital; efforts by Penny Kent of Humphries Press and Theresa Lindsay of the Virginia Institution for the Deaf and Blind; and John Boody who examined the organ give to the hospital by W. W. Cochoron and reported on its condition and history.

My daughter Judy Wood Smith, an experienced geriatrics nurse, has worked with me on a variety of projects for many years. She has helped me decipher an untold number of hand-written letters and papers. Judy also read Stribling's story several times as it evolved, and she made numerous suggestions to improve it.

At a time of crisis, Linda Patrick agreed to create original artwork for the cover, and consequently captured the essence of Stribling's concern for the insane in prisons. Professor Richard Plant made a major contribution to the manuscript late in the process.

For those that I have forgotten, I am sorry.

GLOSSARY

AMUSEMENTS: Pleasurable activities available to patients that improved their mental and physical health.

APARTMENTS: rooms or groups of rooms.

ATTENDANT: Nurse or nurses' aide.

BLACKS OR BLACK PERSONS: Black, colored, Negro, and mulatto were used to describe persons of color during Stribling's time. Some present definitions are "Black," as a person belonging to a dark skinned race: one stemming in part from such a race. "Colored," as a race other than white. "Negro," as people belonging to the African branch of the black race. "Mulattos" as (1) "as the first generation of a Negro and a white" and (2) "a person of mixed Caucasian and Negro ancestry." A large number in those in the Valley were defined in the Census records of the time as "black" or "mulatto." "African" is defined as (1) a native or inhabitant of Africa and also (2) "an individual of immediate or remote African ancestry; esp. Negro. Currently, both black and African-American are often are mingled, sometimes within the same articles.

CARETAKERS: Hospital employees personally caring for the patients or involved in their daily lives such as physicians, attendants, officers and heads of departments, etc.

COURT OF DIRECTORS: Board of directors.

COMMISSION OF INQUIRY AND ADVICE IN RESPECT TO THE SANITERY INTERESTS OF THE UNITED STATES FORCES: The commission co-operated with the Medical Bureau as to the diet and hygiene of troops and the organization of military hospitals.

WESTERN STATE: Replaces various names used for the hospital over the years to describe Virginia's second institution for the insane that was located in Staunton, Virginia.

DIRECTORY: Directors in total.

EASTERN STATE: Replaces several names used over the years to describe Virginia's first institution for the insane located in Williamsburg, Virginia.

HOSPITAL: insane asylum.

INSANE: insane persons: lunatics, mentally ill persons.

KEEPER: Person responsible for the daily, administrative duties of Virginia's mental institutions.

MEMORIAL: Statement of facts addressed to a government often accompanied with a petition or remonstrance's.

MORAL MEDICINE: The totality of treatments that Stribling described as medical and moral means" or therapy with an overlay of the Christian properties that he applied in his practice of both.

MORAL THERAPY: Included as part of "Moral Medicine" in Stribling mss.

ORDINARIES: Inns or hotels.

PHYSICIAN, VISITING PHYSICIAN, CHIEF PHYSICIAN: Until 1841, the head of Virginia's two hospitals for the insane. Physicians at Eastern State did not serve as administrators. Stribling took complete charge of Western State after being elected physician, but allowed Samuel Woodward to keep the title until July 1, 1840 when Stribling made him "steward." The physicians at Eastern State visited the patients as necessary and left its administration to the "keepers." In 1841, the Virginia Legislature changed the law and defined the head of both hospitals as '"Superintendent and Chief Physician." That person had to be a medical doctor and could not engage in private practice. John Minson Galt II was the first person at Eastern State to have the new title.

PRISON DISCIPLINE SOCIETY: An institution that oversaw the treatment of prisoners and reported on their efficiency.

REMONSTRANCE: A Document formally stating points of opposition or grievances.

STEREOSCOPE: An optical instrument with two eyeglasses that allowed the observer to combine the images of two pictures to get the effect of solidity or depth.

SUPERINTENDENTS OR SUPERINTENDENTS' ASSOCIATION: *Association of Superintendents of Insane Asylums.*

WATER CLOSET: a compartment or room for defecation and excretion into a hopper.

HOPPER: a tank holding liquid and having a device for releasing its content through a pipe.

UNITED STATES SANITARY COMMISSION: An umbrella group of relief organizations in New York to help prevent diseases in the army and organize voluntary contributions from the people. With support from Surgeon General of the Army, an official warrant creating the commission was passed on June 9, 1861 and signed by the President on June 18.

GENERAL BIBLIOGRAPHY

Bahr, Lauren S., editorial director, Bernard Johnson, editor-in-chief and Louise H. Bloomfield, executive editor.
Collier's Encyclopedia with Bibliography and Index 8. New York, Toronto, Sydney: (Trademark) Collier's.

Bumb, Jean, "Dorothea Dix." *www.webster.edu/~woolfkm. dorotheadix.htgml;4.*

Blanton, William B. MD. *Medicine in Virginia in the Nineteenth Century.* Richmond, Va.: Garret and Massie. 1933.

Brown, Thomas J. *Dorothea Dix: New England Reformer.* Http/www/hup.harvard.edu/ S98books/S98catalog dix.html.

Bruce, Philip Alexander, LL.B., LL.D. *History of the University of Virginia, 1819-1919: Lengthened Shadow of One Man."* Centennial Edition, vol.2. New York: MacMillan Co.

Central Lunatic Asylum. Board of Directors and Medical Supervisor *Annual Report.* 1870-71: Richmond, Va.

Coleman, Penny. *Breaking the Chain: The Crusade of Dorothea Lynde Dix.* Crozet, Va.: Shoe tree Press, imprint of Betterway Publication, Inc. Congress,

Congress, *First Session of the Forty-first Congress, Private Acts*, 4 March AD1869, 10 April 1869.

Dain, Norman. *Disordered Minds: The First Century of Eastern State Hospital in Williamsburg, Va. 1766-1866.* Williamsburg, Va.: Colonial Williamsburg Foundation. Charlottesville, Va.: Distributed by the University Press of Virginia.

Dix, Dorothea. Letters to Stribling, Staunton, Va.: Western State Hospital.

Driver, Robert. *Civil War Military Records.* Brownsburg, Va.

Druff, Dr. James H. "Francis Taliaferro Stribling Papers at Western State Hospital." Address delivered at the semi-annual meting of the Augusta Historical Society, May 18, 1966 and *Augusta Historical Bulletins* 1-6. Staunton, Va.: Augusta County Historical Society.vol.2 no.2. 19.

Dunn, Nancy Feys. "The Era of Moral Therapy at Western State Hospital." Chicago, MA thesis, De Paul University.

Griffin, Francis Rodgers Huff. *Wagon Roads to Western Mountains of Virginia.* Verona, Va.: McClure Printing Co. 1975.

Hansen, Dr. Hobart G. "Article on Stribling." Received at Western State Library, Dec. 5, 1967: Staunton, Va.: Western State Hospital. 4.

Hurd, Henry et.al. editors. *The Institutional Care of the Insane in the United States and Canada.* Volumes 1-4. Baltimore, Md.: The John Hopkins Press. 1916.

Galt, Dr. John Minson.
"On the Propriety of Admitting the Insane of Two Sexes into the Same Lunatic Asylum." *American Journal of Insanity* 7 (1849-50). "The Farm at St. Anne." *American Journal of Insanity* 10 (1854-55).

Green, E.M., MD. "Psychoses among Negroes, A Comparative Study." *Institutional Care of the Insane* vol.3.

Jarvis, Dr. Edward.
"On the Comparative Liability of Males and Females to Insanity, and Their Comparative Curability and Mortality When insane." *American Journal of Insanity* 7 (1850-51). "Insanity Among the Colored Population of the Free States." *American Journal of Insanity 8* (1851-52).

Lawrence, Charles. *History of the Philadelphia Almshouses and Hospitals*, New York: A New York Times Company. 1876.

Lewis, Jone Johnson, Abstract based on "A Commission of Inquiry and Advice in Respect to Sanitary Interests of the United States Forces," *Encyclopedia of Women's History* and hhtpL/www.netwalk.com/jpr/history1.htmpl.

McIlhany, Hugh Milton, Jr. *Some Virginia Families: Being Genealogies of the Kinney, Stribling, Trout, McIlhany, Millton, Rogers, Tate, Snickers, Taylor, McCormick and other Families of Virginia.* Baltimore: Genealogical Publishing Co. 1962.

McIlhenny, J. J. "The Various Means of Restraints." *American Journal of Insanity* 16 (1850-51).

Moore, Robert L. II. *Chews, Ashby, Shoemaker's Lynchburg and the Newton Artillery: The Virginia Regimental Histories Series, First Edition.* Lynchburg, Va.: H. E. Howard, Inc.

Newspapers, Virginia: (Staunton) *The Vindicator, Staunton Spectator, Valley-Virginian*; (Richmond) *Richmond Inquirer.* (Alexandria) name unknown, *reprinted in Staunton Spectator, Gordonsville Gazette*, reprinted in *Staunton Spectator.*

Powell, Louise Papers. University of Virginia Alderman Library Special Collections: Stribling notes (cards) regarding Medical School at the University of the University; Stribling unpublished correspondence regarding his attempt to obtain a political disability, etc. Charlottesville, VA.

Prison Discipline Society of Boston, Managers. *Annual reports*, Boston: T.R. Marvin. 1826-1854.

Captain Randolph, V.M., U.S.N. *A Candid Inquiry into Some of the Abuses and Cruelties Now Existing and Practiced in the Staunton, Virginia Insane Asylum, Together with A Few Humble Suggestions for Their Correction*, Richmond, Va.: Colin and Nowlan, 1852. Copy. University of Virginia Alderman Library Special Collections.

Rothman, David J. *The Discovery of the Asylum: Social Order and Disorder in the New Republic.*

Boston et.al: Little Brown and Company.

Slave Schedule of Staunton, Virginia. 1860.

Stribling, Francis T.

Annual Reports to Western State Board of Directors. Staunton, Va.: Western State Hospital.

Letters to Dorothea Dix. Houghton Library Harvard University. Cambridge.

"Qualifications and Duties of Attendants on the on the Insane." *Journal of Insanity* 9 (1852-53).

Speech. *Boston Enquirer & Examiner.* June 23, 1868.

Stribling, Frank. Letters to Dorothea Dix, Houghton Library Harvard University: Cambridge.

Stribling, Henrietta. Letter to Frank Stribling. Houghton Library Harvard University. Cambridge.

Stribling Family Bible. Slave births. Mss 779. University of Virginia Special Collections Alderman Library. Charlottesville, VA.

Francis T. Stribling, R.F. Baldwin, Archibald M. Fauntleroy and R. H. Hamilton.

Regulations, Orders, 1854-1883. Staunton,VA. Western State Hospital.

Virginia Legislature. *Doc. No. 1. Governor's Message and annual reports of the Public Officers of the State and of the Board of directors, Visitors, Superintendents, and other agents of public institutions or interest of Va., printed under the Code of Virginia.* William F. Ritchie, Public Printer. 1850. 3.

Waddell, Joseph. *Historical Atlas of Augusta County, Virginia— Maps from Original Survey by Jed Hotchkiss, Top. Engr. Its Annals by Joseph A. Waddell—Physiograply by Jed Hotchkiss, C.& M.E. Illustrated.* Chicago, Ill: Waterman, Watkins &Co. 1885.

Waddell, Joseph, *Annals of Augusta County From 1726 to 1871 by Jos. A.Waddell, Member of the Virginia Historical Society Second Edition 1902*, Harrisonburg, Virginia, Harrisonburg, Virginia: C. J. Carrier Company 1972.

Western State Board of Directors. Annual reports, 1836-1874 Depositions and reports relating to Captain Randolph's charges, miscellaneous letters. Staunton, Va., Western State Hospital. "Investigation of Charges Brought by Captain Randolph Against Western State," January 1853. Staunton, Va.: Western State Hospital.

Wilson, Dorothy Clarke. *Stranger and Traveler, the Story of Dorothea Dix, American Reformer.* Boston-Toronto: Little, Brown and Company.

Woodward, Samuel B., Dr. "Observations on the Medical Treatment of the Insanity," *American Journal of Insanity* 7 (1849-50)

Zwelling, Shormer S. *Quest for a Cure: The Public Hospital in Williamsburg. Virginia, 1773-1885.*Williamsburg: Colonial Williamsburg Publications, 1986.

END NOTES

CHAPTER 1: The Early Years

i   Annual Report of the Court of Directors with Report of the Physician of Western State Lunatic Asylum for 1838, Western State Archives, Staunton, Va. 26.

1.   Annual Report of the Board of Directors, Asst. Physician and Steward of the Western State Lunatic Asylum of Va. for 1873-74, Staunton, Va. 6.

2.   Joseph A. Waddell, *Annals of Augusta County from 1726 to 1871 by Jos. A. Waddell, Member of the Virginia Historical Society Edition 1902*, (Harrisonburg, Virginia. C. J. Carrier & Co. 1986 Second Edition, 17.

3.   Francis Rodgers Huff Griffin, *Wagon Roads to Western Mountains of Virginia, (Verona, VA:* McClure Printing Co.(1975) 57.

4.   Annual Report, 1837. 4.

5.   Annual Report of Western State 1873-74. 6.

6.   *Staunton Vindicator*, July 24, 1874.

7.   Augusta County Deed Book 63-581, June 14, 1839.

8.   Deed Book 64-372, October 1, 1843.

9.   Philip Alexander Bruce, *History of University of Virginia, vol.II, 1819-1919, (New York : Boston McMillan 6)* 106.

10.   Ibid., 111.

11.   Ibid., 107.

12.   Ibid., 114.

13. Ibid., 109.

14. Carol Summerfield and Mary Devine, *International Directory of University Histories*, (Chicago, Il: Fitzroy Dearborn Publishing, 1998.

15. Louis Powell Papers, December 18, 1940, "Cards issued to Stribling by University of Pennsylvania professors, 1830-31," (Charlottesville, Va.: University of Virginia Special Collections Library, Alderman Library).

16. Augusta County Marriage Bond Records, May 17, 1832, Augusta County, Virginia Court House.

17. Stribling Family Bible (Charlottesville, Va.: University of Virginia Special Collections Library, Alderman Library).

18. Shomer S. Zwelling, Quest for a Cure, The Public Hospital in Williamsburg, VA.1773-1885.(Williamsburg, Va.: Colonial Williamsburg Publishing, 1986.) 9.

19. Ibid., 11.

20. Ibid., 3.

21. Ibid., 5.

22. David J. Rothman, *The Discovery of the Asylum*, (Boston-Toronto: Little Brown and Company. xviii.

23. Nancy Feys Dunne, "The Era of Moral Therapy at Western State Hospital," MAA Thesis, De Paul University, 1968, 2-5.

24. Norman Dain, *Disordered Minds, The First Century of Eastern State Hospital in Williamsburg, Virginia*, published by The Colonial Williamsburg Foundation, Charlottesville, VA: University Press of Virginia. 38.

25. Dunne, 5.

26. Ibid., 13.

27. Henry M. Hurd, et. al., *Institutional Care of the Insane in the United States and Canada, vol.* 3, (Baltimore, Md.: the John Hopkins Press, 1916.) 720.

28. Stribling to Dix, March 12, 1859, bMS Am 1838 (613) and bMS Am 1383 (614 and 613A) for paperback, "by permission of Houghton Library, Harvard University," Cambridge, Mass.

29. Hurd, 29.

CHAPTER 2 A Bold New Physician

1. Western State Directors, Report of the Directors, 1873-74, Western State Hospital, 7.
2. Annual Report, 1836, 8-10.
3. Ibid., 8-9.
4. Ibid., 4.
5. Annual Report, 1837, 1.
6. Ibid., 2.
7. Annual Report, 1841, 5.
8. Wyndham B. Blanton, *M.D. Medicine in Virginia in the Nineteenth Century*, Richmond, VA.) Garret and Massie, 1933. 208.
9. Stribling to Dix August 16, 1852, July 19, Houghton Library, Harvard University, Cambridge, Mass.
10. Ibid., July 19, 1850.
11. Frank Stribling to Dix, January 17, 1865, bMS Am 1838 (613a) and bMS 1383 (613A) for paperback, "by permission of Houghton Library, Harvard University, Cambridge, Mass.
12. Annual 1843, 61.
13. Stribling to Directors, 1856.

CHAPTER 3 Stribling Changes Practices, Policies, and Laws:

1. Western State Annual Report, 1840, 18.
2. Annual Report, 1837, 4.
3. Annual Report, 1836, 7.
4. Ibid., 5.
5. Annual report, 1837, 4.
6. Ibid., 5.
7. Francis T. Stribling, R. F. Baldwin, Archibald M. Fauntleroy, and

R. S. Hamilton, "Regulations, Orders, 1854-1883," Staunton, Va., Western State Hospital. 180.

8.   Ibid., 172.

9.   Dr, James H. Druff, "Francis Taliaferro Stribling Papers at Western State Hospital," Augusta Historical Bulletins 1-6, vol. 2, no. 2. (Staunton, VA.: Augusta county Historical Society, 19.)

10.   Dr. Edward Jarvis, M.D, "On the Supposed Increase of Insanity," *American Journal of Insanity 8* (1851-52): 333.

11.   American National Biography, vol.2. 877.

12.   Jarvis, Supposed Increase in Insanity. 333.

13.   Ibid., 363.

14.   Ibid., 356.

15.   Ibid., 361.

16.   Ibid., 355.

17.   Annual Report, 1841, 3.

18.   Shomer S. Zwelling, *Quest for a Cure, The Public Hospital in Williamsburg, Virginia 1773-1885* (Williamsburg, Va.: The Colonial Williamsburg Foundation, 1985) 49.

19.   Nancy Feys Dunne, "The Era of Moral Therapy at Western State Hospital," MAA Thesis, De Paul University, 1968, 30.

20.   Ibid., 31.

21.   *Journal of the House of Delegates of Va., Session 1840-41 (Bill 93), A BILL changing the Existing Laws Relative to the Lunatic Asylums.* Richmond, VA. 42.

22.   Western State Annual Report, 1836, 13.

23.   Report, 1852. 32.

24.   Report, 1850, 35., and 1855, 54.

25.   Report, 1842, 31.

26.   Report, 1842, 55.

27.   Report, 1836, 13.

CHAPTER 4 Life at Western State

1.   Francis T. Stribling, R. F. Baldwin, Archibald M. Fauntleroy, and R. S. Hamilton, "Regulations, Orders, 1854-1883," Staunton, Va., Western State Hospital.

2.   Dr. Luther Bell to Stribling, Nov., 12, 1837. (Attached to 1837 annual report.)

3.   Report, 1837, 24.

4.   Report, 1836, 4.

5.   Report, 1841, 30.

6.   Report, 1843, 36.

7.   Report, 1841, 30.

8.   Report, 1842, 31.

9.   Report, 1836, 4.

10.   Report, 1843, 23.

11.   Report, 1869-70, 34.

12.   Ibid., 35.

13.   Report, 1839. 17.

14.   Report, 1837, 20.

15.   Ibid., 22.

16.   American Journal of Insanity 25 (1868-69): 156.

17.   Report, 1841, 34.

18.   Report, 1852, 104.

19.   David H. Fox, A Guide to North American Organ Builders, (Richmond, Va.) The Organ Historical Society, 1991.) 104.

20.   Report, 1837, 3.

21.   Report, 1843, 23.

22.   American Journal of Insanity, (1857-58): 392.

23.   Report, 1846, 30.

24.   Report, 1871-72 and 1872-73, 31.

25. Stribling, Regulations, 4.

26. Dr. J. J. McIlhenny, "The Various Means of Restraints," American Journal of Insanity 7 (1859-60): 47.

27. Stribling to Dr. Callaway, August 2, 1856, Archives, Western State.

28. Stribling to Thomas Taylor, Oct. 8, 1857.

29. Stribling to B. F. Harris, December 8, 1857.

30. Stribling to Mrs. Bowley, May 15, 1858.

31. Stribling to Mrs. Davis, June 14, 1858.

32. Stribling to mother of patient "Anthony," April 9, 1857.

33. Stribling to Chandler, January 12, 1857.

34. Stribling to Samuel B. Woodward, June 19, 1857.

35. Stribling to Nathaniel Massie, December 17, 1857.

36. Report, 1841, 45.

37. Dr. J. A. Forbes to Stribling, July 27, 1844.

38. Stribling's to Massie, August 23, 1844.

39. Stribling to Massie, September 18, 1844.

40. Norman Dain, *Disordered Minds, The First Century of Eastern State Hospital in Williamsburg, Virginia,* published by The Colonial Williamsburg Foundation, Charlottesville, Va.: University Press of Virginia. 2.

CHAPTER 5 Contention Between Western State and Eastern State

1. Dain. 9.

2. Ibid., 21.

3. Report of the Committee Appointed to Examine the State and Condition of the Lunatic Asylum at Williamsburg, *Journal of the House of Delegates of Va.*, (1834-5 Session, doc.18) 1-3.

4. Henry M. Hurd, et. Al., *Institutional Care of the Insane in the United States and Canada, vol. 3,* (Baltimore, Md.: the John Hopkins Press, 1916.) 711.

5. 1841 bill (93) changing the Existing Laws Relative to the insane. 42.
6. Dain, 70.
7. Managers of the Prison Discipline Society, *Annual Reports*, (Boston: T.R. Marvin, 1826-1854.).
8. Dain, 75.
9. Ibid., 97.
10. Ibid., 138.
11. 1841 bill (93).
12. Annual Report, 1840, 4.
13. Stribling to Galt, November, 1
14. R. Givens Fulton to Stribling, Dec. 12, 1844.
15. Ibid., Dec. 13.
16. Stribling to Fulton, Dec. 18, 1844.
17. Stribling to Committee, Jan. 6. 1845.
18. Dain, 102.
19. Stribling to Sheriff Preston, May 18, 1856.
20. Zwelling, 20.

CHAPTER 6 Dorothea Dix and Dr. Francis T. Stribling—An Intense Friendship

1. Lauren S. Bahr, Editorial director, *(American National Biography, Oxford University Press, 1999 Oxford) 635*
2. Hurd, vol. 1, 120.
3. Jean Bumb, "Dorothea Dix," found at *www.webster.edu/~woolflm/dorotheadix*.htgml 1.
4. Ibid., 4.
5. Hurd, vol. 1. 112.
6. Dorothy Clarke Wilson, Stranger and Traveler, Boston: (Little Brown and Company, 1975): xix.
7. Hurd, 119,
8. *American Journal of Insanity 6* (1850-51): 84.

9.   Bulb, 4.

10.   Stribling to Dix, Jan. ll., 1859, bMS Am 1838 (613) and bMS 1383 (614 and 613A) for paperback, "by permission of Houghton Library, Harvard University," Cambridge, Mass.

11.   Ibid., March 12, 1859.

12.   Dix to Stribling, April 23, 1852, Staunton, Va.: Western State Hospital.

13.   American Journal of Insanity, 1853-54.

14.   Bumb, 4.

CHAPTER 7 Charges of Abuse at Western State

1.   V. M. Randolph, U.S.N. *A Candid Inquiry Into Some of the Abuses and Cruelties Now Existing and Practiced in the Staunton, Va. Insane Asylum, Together With a Few Humble Suggestions for their Correction,* (Richmond Va.: Colin and Nowlan: 1852. Charlottesville, Va.: University of Virginia Special Collections Library.) 2-3. Note: Because Randolph's pamphlet contains 31 pages that have been substantially reduced, this abridgement contains a sufficient number of references to guide future researchers to the source text.

2.   Stribling to Samuel Clark, Oct. 15, 1852.

3.   Randolph's first letter to Dix. (Estimated date, August, 1852.) 18-19.

4.   Ibid., 20.

5.   Ibid., 2¹·

6.   Randolph to Stribing, July 12, 1852. 3.

7.   Ibid., 6.

8.   Ibid., 9.

9.   Stribling to Randolph, July 13, 1852. 6.

10.   Randolph to Stribling, July 19, 1852. 11.

11.   Ibid., 9.

12.   Ibid., 11.

13.   Stribling to Randolph, July 20, 1852.

14. Randolph's "Statement of Facts," 12.

15. Ibid., 15.

16. Ibid., 16.

17. Ibid., 29.

18. Ibid., 30.

19. Ibid., 29.

20. Randolph's second letter to Dix, Sept. 1852. 23.

21. Ibid., 25.

22. Ibid., 26.

23. Ibid., 31.

24. Randolph's first letter to Dix, 22.

25. Court of Directors, Western State Hospital, "Investigation of Charges Brought by Captain Randolph Against Western State, January, 1853," Western State Archives: 15.

26. Deposition by Moses McCowan, Oct. 18, 1852.

27. Depositions by Attendants Patrick McNamara, Caleb Crone, and Samuel Hashour, Dec. 1852.

28. Deposition by Dr. William Hamilton, Dec. 27, 1852.

29. Depositions by Reverends Benjamin Smith and Thomas T. Castleman, late Dec., 1852.

30. Investigating Committee's Report to Directors, "Report of Investigation of Captain Randolph's Charges." 1.

31. Ibid., 4.

32. Ibid., 6.

33. Ibid., 3.

34. Ibid., 10.

35. Ibid., 9.

36. Ibid., 10.

37. Ibid., 11.

38. Ibid., 15.

39. President and Court of Directors' Report to the Virginia Legislature,

"Investigation of Charges Brought by Captain Randolph Against Western State, January, 1853,"Staunton, Va., Western State Hospital.

40. Stribling to Dorothea Dix, March 12, 1853, bMS Am 1838 (613). Houghton Library, Harvard University.

CHAPTER 8 Demise of Moral Medicine in Virginia and Elsewhere

1. Annual Report, 1849, 29.
2. George W. Munsford (on behalf of the Governor Wise) to Stribling, July 1, 1857.
3. Stribling to Governor Wise, January 9, 1857.
4. Annual Report, 1871-72, 31.
5. Dr. John Minson Galt, "The Farm at St. Anne," *American Journal of Insanity*" 10 (1854-55) 352.
6. Ibid., 352.
7. Ibid., 353.
8. *American Journal of Insanity* 12 (1855-56): 42.
9. Ibid., 43.
10. Ibid., 44.
11. Ibid., 45.
12. Ibid., 46.
13. Ibid., 47.
14. American Journal of Insanity 14 (1857-58): 390.
15. Ibid., 391.
16. Stribling to Dix, July 23, 1858, bMS Am 1838 (613), Houghton Library, Harvard University.
17. Dr. John Minson Galt, "On the Propriety of Admitting the Insane of Two Sexes into the Same Lunatic Asylum," *American Journal of Insanity* 11 (1854-55): 224.
18. Stribling to Dix, February 1, 1856, bMS 1838 (613.

19. Stribling to Dix, July 23, 1858, bMS Am 1838 (613).

20. Stribling to Dix, March 12, 1859, bMS Am 1838 (613).

21. American Journal of Insanity 20 (1863-64): 352.

22. Wyndham B. Blanton, *M.D. Medicine in Virginia in the Nineteenth Century*, 208.

23. American Journal of Insanity 22 (1865-66) 524

24. Rothman, 286.

25. Ibid., 269.

26. Ibid., 266.

27. Annual Report, 1871-72, 31.

28. Annual Report, 1873-74, 34.

CHAPTER 9 Treatment of Insane Blacks in Virginia

1. Doc. No. 1, *Governor John B. Floyd's Message and Annual Reports of the Public Officers of the State and Board of Directors, Visitors, Superintendents and Other Agents of Public Institutions of Virginia, Printed Under the Code of Virginia*, Richmond, 1850: William F. Ritchie, Public Printer, 23.

2. Annual report, 1841, 40.

3. Dr. Edward Jarvis, M.D., "Insanity Among the Colored Population of the Free State," *American Journal of Insanity* 8 (1851-52): 268.

4. Hurd, vol. 3, 712.

5. Ibid.

6. Hurd, vol. 3, 711

7. Dain, 110.

8. *American Journal of Insanity* 12 (1855-56): 43.

9. Annual Report, 1848, 34.

10. American Journal of Insanity 30 (1873-74): 178.

11. Stribling, Regulations, 37.

12. Annual Report, 1844, 25.

13. Annual Report, 1846, 30.
14. Western State Directors to Legislature, December, 1852.
15. United States Census, 1860. Slave Schedule.
16. Ibid.
17. Stribling Family Bible, mss 779, (Charlottesville, VA,): University of Virginia Special Collections Library.
18. Alice Wood, "Behind the Iron Gates of Western Lunatic Asylum," News-Virginian, Oct. 17, 1998.
19. Dr. Edward Jarvis, "On the Comparative Liability of Males and Females to Insanity, and the Comparative Curability and Mortality When Insane." American Journal of Insanity 7 (1850-51) 142.
20. Ibid. 162.
21. Annual Report, 1841, 15.

CHAPTER 10 The Civil War Years

1. Waddell, Second Edition, 454, 457.
2. Joseph Waddell, *Historical Atlas of Augusta County, Virginia—Maps from the Original Survey by Jed Hotchkiss, top. Engr. Its Annals by Joseph Waddell—Physiography by Jed Hotchkiss, C. & M.E Illustrated.* (Chicago, Il.): Waterman, Watkins & Co. 1885. 21-22.
3. Ibid., 21-22.
4. Ibid., 23-24.
5. Ibid., 25.
6. Staunton Spectator, December 19, 1962.
7. Waddell 23
8. Ibid
9. Ibid., 24.
10. Ibid.
11. Ibid., 25.
12. Waddell, Second Edition, 498.

13. Regulations, 194

14. Ibid., 75.

15. Ibid., 199.

16. Ibid., 83.

17. Ibid., 84.

18. Annual report, 1863-64.

19. Colonel Robert J. Driver, records on the Civil War.(Brownsburg, Va.) and Robert H. Moore II, Chews, Ashly, Shoemaker's Lynchburg and the Newton Artillery: The Virginia Regimental Histories Series, First Edition, (Lynchburg, VA.) H. E. Howard, Inc.

20. Louise Powell Papers, Stribling Nephew in Baltimore to Cousin Ella Stribling in Staunton.

21. Editor John A. Garraty, American National Biography Vol. 6 NY Oxford University Press 65.

22. Thomas J. Brown, *Dorothea Dix, New England Reformer*, found at http/www/hup.harvard edu/S98books/S98catalog_dix html.

23. Frank Stribling to Dix, December 17, 1864, Bms 1838 Am 1838 (613a) and bMS Am 1383 (614) and (613A) for paperback, Houghton Library, Harvard University.

24. Ibid., January 17, 1838.

25. Mrs. Henrietta Stribling to her son Frank Stribling, December 1, 1864, bMS Am 1838 (613a) and bMS Am 1383 (614) and (613A) for paperback.

26. Hurd, vol. 3, 726.

27. Dain, 166.

28. Ibid., 174

29. Dr. Gray, report to General Foster, *American Journal of Insanity* 20. (1863-64): 351.

30. Dr. Gray's report to General Foster, New York Times, Oct. 31, 1864.

31. The United States Sanitary Commission evolved from several relief societies in New York whose purpose was to aid Federal

soldiers. They obtained the approval of the Acting Surgeon General of the United States Army to become a formal commission.

32.   Gray's article summarized in the American Journal of Insanity, (1863-64): 352.

33.   Civilian Board of Directors of Eastern State to Governor Pierpont, November 1, 1865.

34.   Dain, 190.

CHAPTER 11 After the War

1.   Waddell, 508.

2.   Ibid., 509.

3.   Ibid., 510

4.   Ibid., 514.

5.   Colonel Robert Driver.

6.   Boston, *Enquirer and Examiner newspaper*, June 23, 1868.

7.   John C. Bowyer to Stribling, January 17, 1969.

8.   E. H. Smith to General Butler, February 17, 1869.

9.   Judge Meredith to Stribling, March 6, 1859.

10.   Alfred Chapman to Stribling, March 6, 1859.

11.   *First Session of Forty-first Congress, 1869, Private Acts*, 4 March AD1869, 10 April 1869. 625.

12.   Annual Report 1869-70 and 1870-71, 6.

13.   Ibid., 34.

14.   Ibid., 36.

15.   Ibid., 8.

16.   Regulations, 100.

17.   Ibid., 114.

18.   Ibid., 117.

19.   Annual Report, 1871-72 and 1872-73, 31.

20.   Ibid., 33.

21. Regulations, 101.

22. Annual Report, 1871-72 and 1872-73, 31.

23. Ibid., 9.

24. Annual Report, 1872-73, 34.

25. Rothman, 286.

26. Ibid., 269.

27. Ibid., 266.

28. Annual Report, 1873-74, 5.

29. Staunton, Va., *The Vindicator*, July 24, 1874.

30. *The Richmond Inquirer*, reprinted in *The Vindicator*, July 31, 1874.

31. "Stribling Memorial," *The Southern Churchman*, 1874.

32. Annual Report, 1873-74, 5.

33. *Staunton Spectator*, August 8, 1874.

34. Ibid.

35. *The Vindicator*, July 24, 1874.

36. *Gordonsville Gazette*, reprinted in the *Staunton Spectator*, August 4, 1874.

37. Ibid.

38. Staunton, Va., *The Vindicator, Morning*, July 24, 1874.

39. *The Vindicator*, March 1, 1889.

40. Dr. Hobart Hansen, Superintendent of Western State. Received at Western State Library, December 5, 1967: Staunton, Va.: Western State. 4.

APPENDIX A—Instructions to Western State Employees.

1. Western State By-laws, 1845.

2. Regulations, 91.

3. Ibid., 53.

4. Ibid., 55.

5. Ibid., 20.

APPENDIX B—Superintendents Discuss Restraints.

[1.] Dr. J. J. McIlhenny, "The Various Means of Restraints," American Journal of Insanity 16 (1859-60): 47.

[2.] Ibid., Doctors James L. Anthon and O.C. Kendrick. 50.

[3.] Ibid., Doctors Joseph A. Reed and T.R.H. Smith, 52.

[4.] Ibid., Doctors J. D. Barkdull, John P. Gray and R. Hills, 56.

[5.] Ibid., G.C.S. Choate, 59.

[6.] Ibid., Dr. C. H. Nichols, 61.

APPENDIX C—The Medical Treatment of Insanity as Described by Dr. Samuel B. Woodward

APPENDIX D—Western State Statistics, 1825-1873

[1.] Annual Report, 1872.

APPENDIX E—Insanity in the United States in 1840 Based on the 1840 Census

[1.] Annual Report, 1840, 39.

INDEX